THE SIGNING FAMILY

THE SIGNING FAMILY

What Every Parent Should Know about Sign Communication

DAVID A. STEWART
BARBARA LUETKE-STAHLMAN

CLERC BOOKS
Gallaudet University Press
Washington, D.C.

Figure 12 in chapter 6 reprinted by permission of the publisher,
from G. Gustason and E. Zawolkow, *Signing Exact English*
(Los Alamitos, Calif.: Modern Signs Press, 1993), 7–14.
Figure 20 in chapter 7 reprinted by permission of the publisher, from
H. Bornstein, ed., *Manual Communication: Implications
for Education* (Washington, D.C.: Gallaudet University Press, 1990), 130.

Clerc Books
An imprint of Gallaudet University Press
Washington, DC 20002

*Library of Congress Cataloging-in-Publication
Data*
Stewart, David Alan, 1954–
The signing family : what every parent should know about
communication / David A. Stewart, Barbara Luetke-Stahlman.
p.   cm.
Includes bibliographical references and index.
ISBN 1-56368-06906
1. American Sign Language.   2. Children, Deaf—United States—
Means of communication.   3. Children, Deaf—United States—Family
relationships.   4. Parents of deaf children—United States.
I. Luetke-Stahlman, B.   II. Title.
HV2474.S685   1998
419—dc2198-11618
CIP

Sign illustrations by Lois Lehman

∞ The paper used in this publication meets the minimum requirements
of American National Standard for Information Sciences—Permanence
of Paper for Printed Library Materials, ANSI Z39.48-1984.

Contents

1

MAKING THE DECISION TO SIGN

Why Parents May Want to Learn to Sign

- *Deaf children need to see language in order to acquire it.*
- *Many deaf children find it easiest to communicate in signs.*
- *Many parents use signing to communicate successfully with their deaf child.*
- *Effective communication between deaf children and their parents is important for school achievement.*
- *Signing is one way for parents to show that they accept their child's deafness.*
- *For many children, signing is a valuable first step toward acquiring written and/or spoken English.*

SIGNING—that mysterious purveyor of elusive images. The hands gesticulate, the fingers dazzle. The body hunches, the head bounces. The eyes squint, the shoulders shrug. Little makes sense to you, but you are mesmerized by the swiftness and efficiency of the communication two people create with their hands. You may feel a tinge of envy, much as you do when you hear people speak a different language. Most of us would love to learn another language. But have you ever wanted to learn a signed language?

If your first encounter with signing came at a time when you did not have a deaf child, perhaps you were fascinated but non-chalant about visual language. You may have heard that signing is the backbone of many deaf children's education, but that was of little consequence to you. You may have had no real urge to learn to sign.

Then one day a deaf child came into your life. Suddenly, you were beset with questions for which no amount of schooling or parenting had prepared you. How did you feel then about signing? Did you simply walk into a local college and register for a sign class? Or was your previous fascination with signing pushed aside by fear? Now that you are the parent of a deaf child, you can no longer view signing as an abstraction. You will need to understand what it means for the education and well-being of your child.

Your deaf child forces you to confront difficult questions. Should you give your child the opportunity to learn to sign? If he learns to sign will he ever learn to speak? If she learns to sign, will she be isolated from the hearing world? In this book we will try to help you answer these questions by providing you essential information about signing. Ultimately, you will have to rely on your own feelings. Your decisions will need to be guided as much by intuition as by intellect.

When parents discover their child is deaf, they go through a period of turmoil as they try to respond to a host of concerns. You may hear that signing helps a deaf child acquire language, but, you wonder, don't all deaf people who sign spend most of their social lives in the Deaf community? [Note: We use the term "Deaf" to refer to people who use sign language as their primary means of communication, and who share the culture of the Deaf community. We use the term "deaf" to refer to the larger group of people who have a hearing loss.] Will signing turn your deaf child away from you and the rest of your family? If you do learn to sign, does that commit you to ignoring the vital role of speech and hearing in your child's life? If you don't sign and your child falls behind in school, will you be at fault? What will happen if you try to learn to sign for several years and never become proficient in it?

A large part of this book is devoted to descriptions of various types of signed communication that are used in schools to teach deaf children. At this point we would like simply to introduce the terms for these types of signing, which can be divided into three categories.

- **American Sign Language (ASL)** is the language of the Deaf community and from it the other forms of signed communication have derived the bulk of their sign vocabularies. ASL is a distinct and complete language with a grammatical structure quite different from that of English.
- **English signing** is any type of signing that follows English word order, from haphazard combinations of fingerspelling and signs to formal systems created specifically for coding English in signs. The formal systems are often referred to as **manually coded English** or **MCE.** In this book we discuss two popular MCE systems in detail—**Signing Exact English (SEE)** and **Signed English.**
- **Contact signing** combines ASL signs and some ASL linguistic features with English word order. It formerly was referred to as **Pidgin Sign English** or **PSE.**

WHAT IS SIGNING?

Signing is a visual-gestural means of communication. To say that it is *visual* means that it is perceived through the eye, not the ear. To say that it is *gestural* indicates that signs are formed by the hands within a specific space, called the *signing space.* The signing space for most signed languages encompasses the area between the hips and the top of the head, from the body to the forward and sideways reaches of the hands. A few signs are made outside this space, for example, above the head or below the hips.

The meaning of a sign is determined by four key elements: (1) the

BORED

BITTER

FIGURE 1. The signs BORED and BITTER differ only in their location.

location, (2) the shape of the hand(s), (3) the movement of the hand(s), and (4) the orientation of the palm(s). Changing any one of these characteristics results in the formation of a different sign. The difference between the ASL signs BORED and BITTER is in the location in which they are made (see figure 1). The sign KNOW can be changed to THINK by simply changing the handshape (see figure 2). The signs

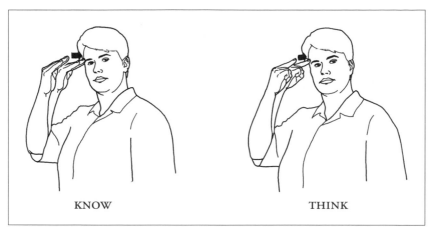

FIGURE 2. The signs KNOW and THINK differ only in their handshape.

FATHER and GRANDFATHER are the same except with respect to movement (see figure 3). In FATHER, the thumb bounces slightly against the forehead, while in GRANDFATHER, the whole hand moves out from the forehead. The difference between THING and CHILDREN is in the orientation of the palm (see figure 4).

The signs formed by the hands are not the sole components of a signed language. That is, not all of the linguistic information that a signer imparts comes from the hands. Just as words convey meaning when embedded in sentences, signs must be arranged according to certain grammatical structures to express a signer's thoughts.

Signing requires skill, and not everyone is adept at it. Learning any language requires more than just the repetition of words or signs. Many people fail a course in a second language because they are unable to learn the vocabulary or grasp the intricacies of a new grammar. Learning to sign presents similar challenges.

Proficiency in a signed language also requires a command of *nonmanual signals*. Spoken languages rely on pitch and intonation to clarify the meanings of words. These features of speech can alter the

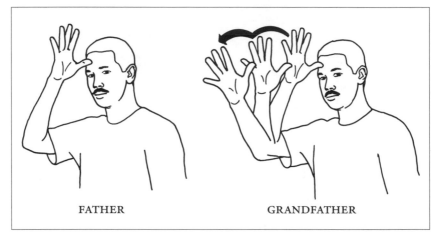

FATHER   GRANDFATHER

FIGURE 3. The signs FATHER and GRANDFATHER differ only in their movement.

meaning of the sentence *You are leaving now* to indicate a command *(You are leaving now!)*, a question *(You are leaving now?)*, a threat *(You are leaving now? That's what you think!)*, or a statement of information *(You are leaving now. The anchor is up.)*. Similarly, signed languages use nonmanual signals to alter the meaning of signed phrases. The head tilts forward and the eyebrows rise or squeeze together when a question is asked. The shoulders sag to express exasperation. The eyes look from one part of the signing space to another to indicate subjects and objects. Nonmanual features of ASL can also be used to express adverbs. The concept of doing something carelessly is expressed by protruding the tongue as if pronouncing the sound "th." For example, forming the adverbial "th" at the same time as signing STUDY is one way of saying that a person is not studying hard. Contact signing and, to a lesser extent, English signing also involve the use of nonmanual characteristics.

Signing is an "in the air, off the body" form of communication. For people accustomed to languages based on sounds, it requires a dramatic shift in thinking. Your ability to make this shift

THING

CHILDREN

FIGURE 4. The signs THING and CHILDREN differ only in the orientation of the palm.

will determine how proficient and effective you are with signed communication.

How Do I Know What Kind of Signing Is Best for My Deaf Child?

Many honest professionals suddenly become cavalier when asked to recommend a form of sign communication. In a very straightforward manner they reply, "Just use American Sign Language with your child because lots of deaf people use it," or, "Your family speaks English, so just use English signs with your daughter." You may even hear people say that it is the *right* of all deaf children to use one type of signing or another. But how could they possibly know what is right for a child without knowing that child and his or her family? These professionals have about as much right to tell you what signs to use as they have to tell you what to name your newborn child. ("Call him Jason. A lot of people call their baby boy Jason.")

Whether you should use ASL, English signing, or contact signing with your child is not a question that we prefer to answer offhandedly. Even if we were your neighbors and knew your child well, we would tread a cautious path in offering advice. Our best suggestion is that you create a set of goals for signing that are centered around the communication needs of your deaf child, and then, by using the information provided in this book, determine how each type of signing maps onto your goals. This process should give you a good idea of what kind of signing you might best like to use with your deaf child.

Signing As a First Step in Communication

For any parent of a deaf child, the foremost goal is communication, and the essential first step is parent-child communication. You want to be able to communicate with your deaf child in much the same way that you communicate with a hearing child of the same age. But remember, we don't always expect 100 percent comprehension the first time we say something to a hearing child. Our expectations with a deaf child should be no different.

Learning to communicate is a step-by-step process. Young children daily add to their ability to ask for things, spin stories, and make sense of their world. They progress from one sign to two signs, from simple sentences to complex sentences, from simple words for complicated ideas to fancy words for simple ideas. Effective communication facilitates language development. How you communicate is going to have a direct impact on how well your deaf child learns a signed and/or spoken language. But it is essential that your child begin to develop language skills during the toddler years.

School is just one of the places where children gain fluency in a language. Many deaf children learn their first language in school, but hearing children acquire fluency in a first language in their own homes. We would like to see deaf children grow up with similar opportunities. Fluent communication between parent and child provides a foundation for whatever language skills the child needs to develop later, including the ability to read and write English. And much of the child's education will hinge on reading and writing skills.

Many deaf children of deaf parents acquire American Sign Language as their first language, and at the same age that hearing children begin to speak. Deaf children of hearing parents generally acquire ASL when they interact with other deaf children who know ASL, an interaction that typically occurs when they begin school in a class of deaf children. Acquiring proficiency in ASL is not a challenge for most deaf children, even though ASL is a complex language. They learn ASL more easily than they learn speech because they can clearly see all aspects of this language. Furthermore, ASL, unlike spoken languages, incorporates the natural dynamics of communication with the hands and body. For this reason, many deaf people consider ASL to be their natural language.

Learning spoken English poses a challenge to a deaf child, and to you as the child's parent. Like all spoken languages, English is sound-based, and sound is something that deaf children have difficulty hearing and understanding. For many of you, signing will be the best way to establish early communication with your child. Many people believe it is also the best way to prepare a deaf child eventually to read and write—and in many cases to speak—English.

HOW SIGNING CAN HELP YOUR DEAF CHILD LEARN ENGLISH

The question of how to make English accessible to deaf children has long baffled their teachers and other professionals in the field. But it is known that deaf children who are exposed to signing at an early age, especially during their toddler years, tend to acquire better reading skills than those who are exposed to signing at a later age. This is because children must have a solid language foundation before they can learn to read in their own, or another, language. What is it about signing that might help your child learn English?

Profoundly deaf children who rely on speech and sound for communication, especially when they are very young, seldom understand the communication around them. It is extremely difficult for them to speechread—to make sense of what little they can hear by watching the lip movements of a language they have not yet learned. But signing is comprehensible to these children because they can see every element of the language. Through daily communication they learn what various hand movements mean and in this way acquire vocabulary and grammar.

Deaf children who sign with their families and others are better able to talk about day-to-day routines—the things they see, the places they visit, the people they meet. Conversation about all of these things makes them more knowledgeable and wiser. These experiences become critical when the children learn to read English. One reason many deaf children who have not learned to sign until they reach school are poor readers is that they lack knowledge of the world.[1] Few have had explained to them why there are different types of motor vehicles, where one state is in relationship to another, or how to use various kitchen utensils. Therefore, the more deaf children are able to communicate, the more information they will acquire, and the more tools they will have for learning how to read.

Here's another way of looking at the relationship between signing and reading. Children must know and be able to express themselves in a language before they can learn to read with comprehension in that language. The larger their vocabulary, the better able the children will be to recognize the printed word once they begin to read.[2] Signing helps them expand their vocabulary—they learn to attach labels to the things they see and talk about. Whether the first language children learn to sign is ASL or English, they are developing language and thinking skills that can be transferred to reading.

WHERE DID SIGNING COME FROM?

In a world obsessed with communication it is surprising to see how little of what we say consists of words or signs. Take these away and you still have a tremendous amount of communication. Nonverbal communication is also a crucial part of everyday conversations.

A nod, a frown, a smile, a shudder all send messages. Nonverbal communication conveys agreement, concern, approval, wariness, and so on. When a teacher turns around suddenly with a stern look, misbehaving students understand that they are being put on notice. A gentle rub on the shoulder communicates affection; a kick under the table warns of dangerous conversational territory.

The use of gestures is not tied to ethnicity or gender. Everyone does it. Infants use gestures as a primary means of communication until their speech muscles are mature enough to articulate meaningful speech. Take away the cultural indoctrination into spoken language and infants might well continue communicating in gestures for the rest of their lives. In time, their gestures might become the building blocks of a language—a signed language. This is not to suggest that signing is the most natural form of communication for human beings, only that it is not *unnatural*. What is unnatural is the taboo that our education system placed on signing for many years.

So the power of your hands to communicate should not come as a surprise. Discovering signing is not like discovering a new language in the heart of the Congo. Signing has always been part of human communication.

For millennia, deaf people have created and used signs among themselves. These signs were the only form of communication available for many deaf people. Within Deaf cultures all over the world, signing evolved to form complete and sophisticated languages. These languages have been learned and elaborated on by succeeding generations of deaf children.

Since the beginning of time Deaf travelers have carried signs across national borders, particularly between countries that shared elements of culture. The signs of England and Australia, for example, are similar because the vast majority of Australia's early European settlers were from the British Isles. The signs of the United States and England, however, are very different. A shared oral language and, to some extent, shared ancestors might have produced similarities in signing, but linguists have found that ASL has more in common with French Sign Language than British Sign Language. (Chapter 2 explains how this happened.) Interestingly, a number of sign languages share some handshapes for the letters of the manual alphabet (though not necessarily for the same letters) or use the same signs for certain objects and concepts.

It is difficult to trace sign languages to a single origin because, like spoken languages, they evolved among deaf people in various places. Until recently, most communities of deaf people maintained their distinctive brands of signing for generations. There can be great variation even within a single country if deaf people from various communities do not mingle. Sign differences can be regional (the signs for AUNT and UNCLE are different in Louisiana and Oregon) or ethnic (some sign variations are unique to deaf African Americans).

In Canada the sign language of most deaf people living in the French-speaking province of Quebec, called Langue des Signes Québécoise, is different from that of the predominantly English-speaking parts of Canada.

Today, regional and group differences are beginning to fade. Affordable air travel brings large numbers of deaf people together for sports events, festivals, and conferences. Sign dictionaries are becoming a part of every deaf person's life, and signing on cable television has helped homogenize sign languages within national borders. Still there will always be regional differences despite the trend to uniformity, much the same as regional dialects will always exist in spoken languages.

SIGNING AND PARENTING

In an authentic signed conversation between two deaf people, there is hardly an opportunity for you to cut in and announce sheepishly, "Hey, I'm just learning to sign." You struggle to catch a sign here and there, but the conversation swirls on. Signing is the lifeblood of communication for the conversants and they just charge ahead with it.

Most parents of deaf children know only fingerspelling and a few signs. To become proficient signers, both parents and children need role models such as Deaf adults, older deaf children who are fluent signers, and other parents who have learned to sign well. Your best role models may be the people who inspired you, either directly or indirectly, to open your home and heart to sign.

You want to sign the way Deaf people do so that the conversation in your home can flow freely. You arm yourself with a course or two and set off into the Deaf community. But they sign so fast! And they can talk about anything and be understood. "Oh," you think, "that's what our family needs." There is no dimension of thought that cannot be expressed through signing. That's one of the keys for you in choosing to sign with your deaf child—you want unhindered communication with your child.

Once you learn some type of signing, don't get flustered by its speed in the hands of expert signers. Marvel at its beauty, its effectiveness. Be content with the thought that one day soon, you will be able to explain something to your child and she or he will understand. You will be able to offer genuine, comprehensible praise. You will be able to read to your child before bedtime and the story will be treasured.

One day, many of you will be fluent signers. If you have a very young child, perhaps you have already begun using a few signs as tools for communicating and learning, for socializing and playing. If your child is old enough to know how to sign but struggles with speech to communicate with you, perhaps you want to move closer to the child by learning an alternative form of communication. Even if your deaf child is a successful speechreader and doesn't sign at school, perhaps you have heard that many deaf adults who were educated in the oral method learned to sign as teenagers. You and your older child may now want to learn, too.

Tools have a purpose in our lives. Signing, as a tool, helps us to communicate with our children. Through signing you will be able to explain clearly about family traditions, your religious beliefs, why your pet had to be put to sleep, and why Mom and Dad need their sleep on Saturday morning!

Signing also leads to a command of language, and for many profoundly deaf children it does so a lot more effectively than speech. However, it takes time to learn to sign, and signing, in and of itself, does not guarantee that your child will succeed in school. When you learn to sign you must not forget about being a parent and doing all of the other things that will help your child to learn.

Signing does allow you to tell your deaf son to go brush his teeth. But it doesn't mean that he will. With signs, you can clearly and eloquently explain nuclear fusion to your deaf daughter, but that doesn't mean she will understand it. A deaf child's intelligence and need for love cannot be nursed on signing alone. Parenting is a complicated task, no matter what mode of communication you use.

If you decide that learning to sign is right for your family, remember that there is no quick and easy way of doing so. There is no Minister of Sign, who for a few dollars and a signature will perform the rites that turn you into a proficient signer. Learning to sign is not as easy as many people suppose. Indeed, this misconception is shared by many professionals. Some university programs send teachers into the field to teach deaf children after just a course or two in signing. And we have heard of people taking positions as sign instructors after completing only beginners' sign courses! Learning to sign proficiently takes as much time and practice as the learning of any other language.

THE INSECURE PARENT

Many parents get frustrated communicating with their children, whether the children are deaf or hearing. When the parents of a deaf child are not fluent signers, their sense of inadequacy as communicators can make them feel uncomfortable with their deaf child. While it is good for parents to be reflective about their relationships with their children, these feelings of inadequacy should not divert them from whatever task is at hand.

Jan and Scott are good examples of parents who allow their limitations in signing to interfere with their roles as parents. Jan is cheerful, outgoing, and respectful of other people. Scott is more withdrawn; at social gatherings he is inclined to stay in the background while his wife mingles. They have a seven-year-old deaf daughter named Kate and a six-year-old hearing daughter named Kristen. Their expectations of the two girls are remarkably different. After a presentation by a deaf person to a group of parents of deaf children, Jan and Scott watched the girls socializing in the crowd. Kristen was expected and even prodded by her parents to say hello to people and tell them something about her school activities or what she was doing with her spare time. Her parents kept an eye on her and often joined her in conversation while she skimmed in and out of this linguistically rich social activity.

The treatment of the deaf daughter contrasted sharply with that of her hearing sister. Scott kept an eye on Kate, asking now and then if she wanted a cookie or a drink. (COOKIE is the first sign many parents learn, perhaps during snack-time when the parent educator comes to visit. Eager to use their newfound signing skills, they ask, "DANNY, YOU COOKIE?" We are waiting for the day when Danny looks up quizzically and replies, "Gee, no Mom, I am not a cookie." But let's not get sidetracked.)

Hearing fathers are usually the poorest signers in the family, if they can sign at all. Scott is no exception. Jan, who has a fair grasp of signing, did attempt to bring Kate into conversations. One such attempt with a deaf man who was a fluent signer began this way: "Kate, tell him how old you are." Not "tell him about your school activities" or "tell him about your horse collection," as Jan would have said to Kristen, the younger sister. Kate signed "AGE SEVEN" and was ready to gallop off, but the man held her back to learn more. Kate's delightful personality unlocked when she realized that the man could sign. With access to social conversation, Kate told him about her hobbies, projects at school, and plans for the coming weekend.

Jan and Scott wanted their deaf daughter to take part in this social event, but both were afraid to start a prolonged conversation that might reveal their embarrassing weakness in signing. How much richer Kate's experience would have been, linguistically and socially, if Jan had introduced her to people in a manner more conducive to conversation: "Kate is finishing a project for school that is really exciting. Kate, what did you think was the best part of your project?" This is communication, wrapped in the fabric of socializing. To be able to explain and describe your world, model social conversation, and allow your child to participate—aren't these the reasons to learn to sign?

SIGNING IN SCHOOL

Most parents evaluate the option to sign in terms of their child's access to education. Legions of Deaf people will attest to the fact that their education accelerated after they learned to sign. This effect is particularly common among deaf children who are placed in an oral environment for the early years of their schooling. The oral method may be appropriate for some deaf children, but for many others, learning barely moves forward because of the time spent repeating spoken phrases. Historically the inability to master oral communication has limited many deaf children's access to the information typically taught in school.

Learning to sign does not guarantee a better education. It does open doors to learning, however, because for deaf children signing is a more comprehensible form of communication than speech. This premise is clarified in later chapters, which explore the role of signing in the education of deaf children during the past two centuries.

Despite a long history of signing in the United States, many school districts still lack adequate instruction in signing. Even if your school district provides good instruction, it may not subscribe to the type of signing you want for your child. It is possible to advocate for your chosen method of communication and win, although in such disputes the law in most states favors the schools. In chapter 9, we discuss the law and how you can use it to your advantage. We don't promise that it will be easy, and we can't guarantee that you will always get what you want.

MAKING THE DECISION TO SIGN

For many parents, discovering that their child is deaf is a traumatic experience. It destroys their previous notions of how their child will develop, go to school, have friends, visit grandparents, attend college, and so on. Above all, it puts a damper on the parents' expectation of hours and hours of conversation with their child where they share their experiences and dreams. Some parents never recover from the shock to realize that their child can, in fact, do all of these things. They never accept their child's deafness or recognize the child as a capable individual who will experience the pains and joys of growing up just as other children do.

While there have to be some differences in our expectations for a deaf child, we must remember that our society is filled with differences in culture, income, geography, and so on. The reality is that we do not expect all children to be raised in the same manner. But we should expect that all children have access to those things in life that are necessary to fulfill their fundamental needs. We are all motivated to know what is going on around us, why things happen, and what effect events have on our lives. To access such information we must be able to communicate, which leads to the ability to think, react, and analyze the world.

In considering whether or not to sign with their child, parents should be careful not to be influenced by attitudes that now are outdated. Not so long ago, the conventional view outside the Deaf community was that if you couldn't speak, you didn't have a language. And if you didn't have a language, you couldn't be intelligent. This myth was powerful among many linguists and educators in the last part of the nineteenth century and for much of this century. Proponents of the oral-only approach to language development latched on to this way of thinking, forbidding the use of sign language and allowing only speech and speechreading as the mode of communication. For a long time parents everywhere, deaf and hearing, were wrongly convinced that their deaf children had to learn to speak at the expense of learning school subjects. Where did this leave the Deaf adults who signed? They were wrongly accused as being semi-literate gesture makers. True, they could string signs together, but was it language? According to the thinking of those times, signed language was not considered as complex as spoken language and, therefore, was viewed as inferior.

Today, the theory that only speech leads to language acquisition has been discarded. Signing does lead to language development, and for many profoundly deaf children, it is the best route to reading and writing proficiency.

Deaf children need to communicate. Through effective communication, which leads to language, they will be able to learn, work, contribute to society, and enjoy life as much as anyone. While we realize that not everyone will learn to sign, we do know that more and more people are in fact learning how to sign. American Sign Language is one of the fastest-growing languages of study in the United States.

The past two decades have ushered in a greater awareness of who Deaf people are and how they communicate. It is no longer unusual to see people signing. Deaf people who sign are making their mark in the world. Marlee Matlin won an Oscar for her performance in "Children of a Lesser God," Heather Whitestone captured the hearts of the nation as Miss America, and Linda Bove has introduced thousands of children to sign language on *Sesame Street.* Thousands of other deaf people who sign are not well known, and rightfully so—because being deaf and signing your way through life is not such a big deal. Why should it be? Many deaf people have used signing to carve a niche in this world as teachers and professors, doctors and chiropractors, lawyers and members of the court, engineers and construction workers. Making the decision to sign with your child is the first step toward his or her eventual success.

NOTES

1. Paul and Quigley 1994.
2. Paul 1996.

2

SIGNING IN THE EDUCATION OF DEAF CHILDREN

> ### *What Parents Should Know about Signing and Teaching*
>
> ◆ *Signing has played a formal role in the teaching of deaf children in the United States since the first school for deaf children opened in 1817.*
> ◆ *All forms of signing have had some success in the teaching of language and academic subjects to deaf children.*
> ◆ *There has always been controversy about which type of signing is best to use in teaching.*

IF ENOUGH PEOPLE repeat an idea—even if it is not true— it eventually takes on the appearance of being true. The statement "If you sign, your child won't learn to speak" has no support in research. Yet in the minds of many teachers and parents, it has become an unquestioned fact. The field of deaf education is full of myths, especially about signing. As authors, we hesitate even to dispute them because in doing so we give them more attention than they deserve.

To sign or not to sign? This question has plagued parents for centuries, and it is likely to plague them well into the next century. Our best answer is to point out that all deaf children are unique. If your child is happy, has friends, and is making academic prog- ress on a level with other children of the same age, you must be doing something right. If not, perhaps it is time for you to learn to sign, or to sign more proficiently, or to change the type of signing you use.

It can be said with perfect honesty that thousands upon thousands of deaf children have succeeded in education systems that espoused signing. If signing students have enjoyed so much success, why don't all deaf children learn to sign at an early age? Why don't all schools with programs for deaf children advocate signing? One reason is that some deaf children can learn and socialize without signing, and their parents are very proud and vocal about their children's abilities. But most deaf children cannot obtain the education level they are capable of or be truly included in social conversations without signing. We cannot repeat too often that signing does not keep children from learning to speak. Many signing children have excellent speech. Signing is simply one of many communication tools at their disposal. The awareness is growing among teachers and parents that the more tools children have in their tool boxes, the more successful they will be in learning and socializing.

Consider this example, which is far from unique. We know a deaf woman whose first language as an infant was sign language, and later she learned to speak, read, and write fluently in English. She worked her way through graduate school and got a job at a major state university. She accomplished this having parents and a sibling who are also deaf. The members of the family all move freely between American Sign Language (ASL) and signing in English in their day-to-day communication.

Stories like this tackle not only the number one myth about signing—that if a deaf child learns to sign he or she will not learn to speak—but also the tagalong myths that the child will have trouble learning to read and write English and will never be gainfully employed. This deaf woman has the tools for communicating and interacting with others, and she also has an excellent education. She is not alone. Many deaf people have used signing to get a good education and to prepare for life. We hope that this book will inspire you to cast aside unproductive myths. Signing is not only a viable option but a good one for most deaf children.

HOW DOES SIGNING FIT INTO A DEAF CHILD'S EDUCATION?

About one child in every thousand has a hearing loss that is severe enough to hamper the comprehension of speech even with the use of a hearing aid. With such a small number of deaf children to concern us and a good two hundred years of experience in teaching them, one would think that their education would be standardized nationwide. But deaf children's needs are highly diverse, and schools have developed a range of programs to meet them.

Factors That Influence a Child's Educational Needs

Even children with similar degrees of hearing loss arrive at school with varying levels of preparedness. This is due, in part, to the children's ages at the onset of deafness and the kinds of support available to them at home.

Age at Onset of Deafness. The apparently simple matter of the age at which a child becomes deaf is in fact critical because it determines the child's degree of exposure to spoken language. Children who become deaf at the age of two or later are called *postlingually* deaf. These children have already started speaking and have acquired language skills that will assist in the further development of language as they adjust to being deaf and to learning a new communication mode.

Children who are born deaf or become deaf before they learn to speak are called *prelingually* deaf. They cannot experience sounds in a manner that facilitates the acquisition of speech. Many of them do not hear speech well enough to acquire a spoken language even after the hearing loss is discovered and they are fitted with hearing aids.

They must rely on visual modes of communication such as signing, speechreading, and print.

Family Support. The most fundamental form of support is parents' acceptance of the fact that their child is deaf. This doesn't come easily for many hearing parents. The birth of a child brings with it much joy and hope. Parents have high hopes that the child will become an avid reader, a skilled athlete, an exceptional musician, or a fine artist. More commonly, parents hope that their child will be happy, have friends, enjoy school, get a job, marry, and be liked by others. When they find out that their child is deaf, their dreams for the future are at least temporarily lost in the onslaught of new emotions. Grief, anxiety, anger, and guilt permeate everyday thoughts as the parents struggle to adjust to a new reality. What was once taken for granted becomes questionable.

However long this painful period lasts, parents do not truly leave it until they have accepted their deaf child as he or she is. Parents must realize that a hearing loss does not mean loss of hope. All of their original hopes for the child should have a role in the new reality. The main difference in raising a deaf child is providing for communication and learning experiences oriented to a world of seeing rather than hearing. Having arrived at this understanding, parents are prepared to nurture the intellectual growth of their child. Exposure to Deaf cultural activities is a valuable part of the process. Making the child part of the parents' world, however, is the essential first step.

Parents show their support in other ways. They may decide to learn to sign, or they may embark on an extensive speech training program with their child. In any case they should start early and maintain a high level of involvement in the child's education. For example, if they send their child to a school for deaf children, they should not assume that this relieves them of responsibility for communicating with the child at home. If they send their child to a public school program, they should make sure that the child receives appropriate services. It is important for parents to appreciate their child's abilities and to provide the encouragement and support necessary for maximizing these abilities, just as they do for their hearing children. And parents should keep grandparents and siblings involved—it is important for a deaf child to be fully included by everyone in the family.

Types of School Programs

The reason there is a range of programs for deaf children is that each type is best for some children. A child who succeeds in one program might perform below his or her potential in another. Poor performance does not necessarily indicate poor schooling. Parents must take an active part in their child's education to ensure that the school program is doing all that can be done to provide the learning environment that is best for the child.

The two main factors in your choice of an educational program are the type of school and the communication methodology used. You will need to choose either a school devoted exclusively to deaf education or a public school with an appropriate program for deaf children. Many schools for deaf children are also residential. But children who live nearby may attend on a daily basis, going home after school. Children from farther away sleep in a dormitory or a group home. Almost all of these children go home for weekends. This preserves family ties and encourages parents to stay involved in their child's education. Schools for deaf children are greenhouses of Deaf culture and are especially well suited to help children attain fluency in ASL.

In public schools deaf children are taught either in general education classrooms with their hearing peers or in self-contained classrooms with teachers certified to teach deaf children. In a general education classroom deaf children may have access to sign language interpreting services and other support services as needed. A self-contained classroom in a public school, like the classrooms in schools for deaf children, usually has four to seven children. The children may be integrated for part of the day in general education classes such as mathematics and social studies.

Programs differ in the communication methodologies they offer. Most programs offer a *total communication* approach, which includes the use of signs, speech, audition, and other means of communication, with English as the language of instruction. The philosophy of total communication is that the teacher should use the form of communication that best fits a child's educational needs—that is, the form best understood by the child. In many classrooms, this means that the teacher signs and speaks at the same time, a method known as *simultaneous communication.* Contact signing is used in most of these programs; some require their teachers to use a particular system of manually coded English. In some self-contained classrooms the teachers use ASL, and in nearly all schools for deaf children ASL is used by some of the teachers, in varying degrees, and is known by most of the students. A handful of schools for deaf children and a small number of public school programs embrace a *bilingual-bicultural* approach, a recent development in the field. In a bilingual-bicultural classroom, Deaf culture plays a primary role in shaping the curriculum and the language of instruction. One version of the bilingual-bicultural program (called Bi-Bi) requires that ASL be used for all signed communication; English is taught as a second language to develop reading and writing skills. Other programs use various combinations of ASL and English signing.

Visit your local school program and the schools for deaf children in your state to see what they have to offer for your child. If you live in a rural or remote area, check into educational cooperative programs as well. Find out what the communication policies are in each program and the extent to which teachers and administrators adhere to the policies. Satisfy yourself that the program you choose will provide adequate support services to optimize your child's learning.

Who Decides What's Best for a Deaf Child?

Parents, of course, are responsible for deciding what is best for their child. Once the child turns three, however, teachers, administrators, and other professionals become involved in deciding what is best for the child's education. Teachers reach out to their students through communication. And teachers, by nature, are a resourceful group! Time has taught them that most means of communication are successful with at least some deaf children. This has led to great variety in the instructional repertoire of teachers of deaf children. Many deaf children have been instructed in several communication modes, and a small number have also learned the hand signals for cued speech.[1]

We might wish to believe that it is the needs of the child that determine the kind of communication to be used with him or her in school. But history shows that the preconceptions of teachers or parents have the most weight. Teachers and parents do what they think is right (or what the group they associate with thinks is right), and being human, they also tend to do what is convenient. The choice of communication modes in the classroom typically falls on the shoulders of the teachers, who are inclined to continue communicating as they have in the past. Public school administrators usually lack strong opinions about teaching practices with deaf children. Very few have studied deafness, let alone established a sign policy for their program.

By far the two most common means of communication used in school programs for deaf children are signing and speaking. They may be used either separately or together. Which one prevails in the teaching of a particular child depends on a number of factors, such as the child's degree of hearing loss and ability to acquire a signed or spoken language, the parents' preferred mode of communication, the parents' willingness to sign, and the skills of teachers. Of course, it also depends on the approach endorsed by the school or the district or state where the school is located. Some states have a strong tradition in oral education.[2] Many of the programs for deaf children in those states advocate an oral education and use very little signing, if they allow it at all. On the other extreme, some school programs that emphasize signing offer little or no speech training.

Parents' preferences are often culturally linked. A deaf parent's desire that his or her deaf child learn ASL and a hearing parent's choice of spoken English both are examples of cultural influence. Sometimes parents are unduly influenced or even intimidated by the status of professionals who give them advice. Even the opinion of a knowledgeable professional should be regarded as one factor among many in the decision process. And parents should be particularly wary of the advice of professionals who have no expertise in deaf education. One family's dentist questioned their use of signs and advised them to use speech alone with their deaf children. We can only guess why this dentist was numb to his own unfitness to give such advice. When he repeated his views at each visit, the family switched dentists.

What we have just said about the education of deaf children may seem confusing and disheartening to parents. It need not be. Parents have a tremendous influence on how well their children learn, and there is much that they can do.

A BRIEF HISTORY OF DEAF EDUCATION

We now turn to the history of signing in the education of deaf children in the United States. We take a rather broad sweep so as to capture the essence in a small space.

Deaf education and sign language have been intimately linked since the founding of the first permanent school for the deaf in the United States. The Connecticut Asylum for the Education and Instruction of Deaf and Dumb Persons officially opened its doors on April 15, 1817, in Hartford, Connecticut.[3] Thus began the first attempt in the United States to provide a formal education for deaf children within the confines of a state-funded institution. The school's main mode of communication was signing. Speech may also have been part of the curriculum, but historical reports are vague on this point.

The school's founder, Thomas Hopkins Gallaudet, was a young minister from Connecticut. He had been asked by a wealthy physician, Dr. Mason Cogswell (who had a deaf daughter) and others to travel to Europe to learn about teaching deaf children. With no pre-conceptions about which form of communication might be best, he ventured forth to learn what he could.

His first destination was the Braidwood Academy in Edinburgh, Scotland, which subscribed to the oral-only approach to teaching. Initially, the Braidwoods were reluctant to teach Gallaudet their method, but they finally offered him an apprenticeship with the conditions that he stay with them for several years and that he keep their methods a secret. Gallaudet rejected their offer. While in London, he chanced upon a meeting with the Abbé Sicard, the director of the Royal Institution for the Deaf in Paris. Sicard invited Gallaudet to visit the school, which he did and there he encountered deaf children being instructed in signs. The Royal Institution used Methodical Signs, which was a way of coding French into signs. It resembled some present-day English-based systems except in being based on French.

Before returning home Gallaudet recruited a deaf teacher from the institution, named Laurent Clerc, to accompany him. On the voyage back to the United States, Clerc taught French Sign Language to Gallaudet, and Gallaudet taught English to Clerc. The two became the founders and first teachers of the Connecticut Asylum, which began with just seven students ranging from twelve to fifty-one years of age. Thirty-three students were enrolled the following year.[4] The Connecticut Asylum is still in existence today and is known as the American School for the Deaf.

During the next fifty years, twenty-five more schools for deaf children were established in the United States. The apex of this movement was the establishment of the National Deaf-Mute College (later renamed Gallaudet College and then University) in 1864. In 1867 the first oral school for deaf children, later known as the Clarke School for the Deaf, was established in Northampton, Massachusetts. It is worth noting that twenty-six schools for deaf children were teaching in signs before the first oral school opened its doors.

The Early Days of Signing in Schools

What kind of signing did teachers of deaf children use when deaf education was new in the United States? Gallaudet and Clerc borrowed the Methodical Sign method used in France and incorporated the sign language used by American deaf people at that time. They also used fingerspelling and writing. Methodical Signs followed the word order of spoken French. Even today ASL uses some French constructions, and some ASL signs have handshapes derived from the manual representation of the first letters of French words, such as *autre* and *cherchez* (for OTHER and SEARCH).

It is unlikely that when they returned to the United States Gallaudet and Clerc used Methodical Signs exactly the way they had learned them in France. Being a native Frenchman and deaf, Clerc knew how to sign in French Sign Language (FSL).[5] We can reasonably assume that in teaching he combined his knowledge of both FSL and Methodical Signs with his growing knowledge of English and the signs that his American students brought to school.

Gallaudet, on the other hand, was a hearing person whose native language was English. Methodical Signs was the first sign system he encountered, although he also learned aspects of FSL from Clerc. Certainly he was influenced by the principles of Methodical Signs, FSL, and his native English language. But Gallaudet could hardly have been a proficient signer when he arrived back in America.

The teaching of Gallaudet and Clerc was the beginning of their influence on the vocabulary and grammar of ASL. This influence was spread by their students, who combined whatever signs they were already using—homemade signs or signs from the Deaf community—with the ones they learned in school. Likewise, the teachers adopted signs their students used. The signs that made it into the daily routines of the classroom and traveled back home to various Deaf communities were those deemed to be the most appropriate by the most people. In time, this way of signing evolved to become present-day ASL.

Signing Goes by the Wayside

By 1880 the vast majority of deaf children in the United States were being taught in signs in state-run residential schools. About half of all teachers of deaf children were deaf. These teachers were instrumental in establishing signing as the primary means of communication in these schools. The influence they exerted on their deaf students had a tremendous effect in shaping the signing behavior of Deaf communities everywhere in the United States. Thus, there was a strong connection between the signing used inside and outside the schools.

Despite this favorable situation for signing, things began to change. Just as signing was making its way into the lives of most deaf children, a movement began with the aim of assigning speech a more prominent role in deaf children's education. The oral movement was especially strong in Europe. Everywhere it appeared, the rationale was that speech is indispensable if a child wishes to be a part of society. In 1880 a group made up primarily of European educators issued a resolution that endorsed the use of speech and the banning of signing as the preferred means of instruction for deaf children. This action took place at the Second International Congress on the Education of the Deaf in Milan, Italy. Among the two hundred professionals present was only one deaf person.

Although the American contingent of educators did not approve of the Milan resolution, they were powerless to prevent its lasting effect over time. In the United States oralism gained momentum through the work of Alexander Graham Bell, who advocated educating deaf children in oral day schools and adamantly opposed residential schools and the use of sign language. The result of the Milan resolution and the work of Bell and other oral advocates was a complete overhaul of the communication methods used in American deaf education. Thirty years after the resolution, nearly all school programs were committed to providing their deaf children with an oral education. In 1907 there were 139 schools for deaf children in the

United States and none of them accepted ASL as an official means of instruction.[6] The number of deaf teachers had fallen from about 50 percent to below 15 percent because teachers were being hired for their ability to teach orally. This situation persisted from the 1880s through the late 1960s.

Signing did not disappear completely from the schools, despite the severe punishments associated with it. (As recently as the 1960s, deaf students had their hands strapped or were forced to place them under their legs when caught signing. Deaf adults will confess to myriad strategies they used as schoolchildren to circumvent nonsigning policies. One favorite was to fingerspell behind their backs to classmates sitting behind them.) In most residential settings students were free to sign after school hours. Children who didn't know how to sign learned from those who did, especially from those who had deaf parents (and this still happens at the large oral schools). The few deaf teachers who managed to obtain employment in the education system taught mainly in residential schools for deaf children. Perhaps because they used signs, their presence was often viewed as detrimental to the teaching of speech. Consequently, most taught at the high school level where the focus was academics, not speech training.

What did we learn from nearly a century of deaf education dominated by the oral approach? We discovered that most deaf children did not acquire intelligible speech and many failed academically.[7] We discovered that you cannot prevent deaf children from using signs when they want and need to engage in meaningful and complex communication. And we discovered that early access to signed communication was linked to superior academic performance. We concluded that signing plays an important role in the education of deaf children.

The Rebirth of Signing

What happened in the 1960s that caused teachers to take a second look at signing as a viable means of communication in schools?

There was a growing concern among educators and parents that most deaf children were not succeeding academically as well as their hearing peers. Moreover, many deaf children still had unintelligible speech even though they spent much of their school day being trained to speak. But there were too few school programs that used signing to allow for an in-depth comparison of teaching methods. Researchers needed to find a group of deaf children who had consistently used signing outside the classroom. Deaf children of Deaf parents who used signing as their main mode of communication at home and in the community fit the bill.

Study after study began to show that deaf children of Deaf parents were doing better in school, had better social skills, and had better self-images than deaf children of hearing parents who were in oral programs. And the clincher? There was no significant difference between the speech of deaf children of Deaf parents and that of deaf children of hearing parents. This isn't to say that the speech skills of either group were acceptable—just that there was no evidence that signing hindered speech development.

What greatly concerned parents and school personnel was that deaf children of Deaf parents still lagged considerably behind their hearing peers in all academic measures. Moreover, although they achieved academically at a higher rate than deaf children of hearing parents, the gap in achievement was not a cause for celebration: It amounted to only about one grade level in mathematics and reading.[8] Still, the studies conducted in the 1960s were effective in getting people to take another look at signing. Speech-driven education was challenged and ultimately nudged to the side by a newfound appreciation of the benefits of signing.

The Many Shades of Signing

Timing makes all the difference in so many transformations. Just as studies began to demonstrate the benefits of exposure to signed communication, a Gallaudet University professor, William Stokoe, published a pioneering linguistic analysis of ASL. No longer were deaf signs viewed as "broken English," a haphazard collection of signs. Stokoe showed that Deaf people have a true language that parallels the richness of oral languages.

But the structure of ASL was still foreign to many teachers, and very little had been written to help them understand it. They were faced with a big question: "How do you go about using ASL to teach English when their grammatical structures are different?" The education system was still dominated by an orientation to English and therefore leaned strongly toward a type of signing that was more like English than ASL. This orientation was not limited to hearing teachers. Many deaf teachers at the time also supported the use of English as the primary language of the classroom. In the 1960s professionals in the field simply were not prepared to venture into new territory and use ASL for instructional purposes.

Total Communication: The Door Opener

Before signing could be officially welcomed into schools, there had to be a new philosophical stance to replace oralism. Total communication answered the call. First articulated by Roy Holcomb, a deaf teacher and parent of two deaf children, the total communication philosophy became the banner for schools that wanted to use signing to teach deaf children. Originally it called for the use of whatever forms of communication worked best: signs, speech, audition, print, or any combination of these. It was intended to be a child-centered approach that would require teachers to assess the communication needs of each student and respond accordingly.

In practice, total communication became associated with the concurrent use of signs and speech known as *simultaneous communication,* or SimCom. Because most teachers of deaf children were hearing, they used speech to guide their signing rather than vice versa. As a result, the signs they used were arranged in English word order. In this way simultaneous communication presented English in two modalities. It became the goal of total communication programs to expose deaf children to English in signs and speech throughout the school day.

By 1980 about two-thirds of deaf children in the United States were being educated in total communication programs. This represented a remarkable turnaround for a field that had been almost completely dominated by oral programs just ten years earlier. Total communication was the mechanism for bringing signs into the classroom, but what signs did it bring?

Manually Coded English: The First Step

In reviewing the history of total communication we must bear in mind that for most people in the 1960s and '70s, signing was a strange and exotic way of communicating, and ASL was not accorded the respect that other languages received. Deaf adults who used signs were ostracized by many people outside the Deaf community. Research into ASL had just begun and what little we did know about ASL was confined to a small circle of researchers and other interested professionals. Since neither deaf nor hearing teachers knew how to teach ASL grammar, they were uncertain as to the benefits that exposure to ASL might present to deaf children learning English as a second language. And parents were apprehensive about the use of ASL in the classroom. One thing teachers did realize was the impossibility of signing in ASL and speaking English at the same time. For this reason, ASL was not regarded as a viable option for total communication programs.

The question then became, "How do we incorporate signs into the school program?" Advocates of total communication tackled this problem in much the same way the French had done with Methodical Signs: They decided to create a new sign system. It was clear that to sign and speak simultaneously, a signer would have to use signs or fingerspelling for each word, or at least for many of the words spoken. Although Deaf people had done this when communicating with hearing people who signed, no standardized system existed for conveying English in signs. Educators agreed it would be advantageous to use ASL signs even if the grammar of ASL was not part of a newly created sign system. A group of educators, other professionals, parents, and deaf people set out to create the methods of signing that became known as manually coded English (MCE).

MCE systems were created for three main reasons. First, there are many words and morphemes (meaningful parts of a word) in English for which ASL does not have a sign. This disparity between signs and speech does not mean that ASL has a limited vocabulary. Many signs have multiple meanings, and fluent signers are able to convey all concepts effectively in signs. The MCE developers focused their efforts on creating one-to-one English/sign correspondence to improve deaf children's reading proficiency. This involved inventing signs for parts of English such as articles (*a, the*), the verb *to be (is, are, am, be),* and affixes (tense endings, prefixes, suffixes). The MCE developers also hoped that exposing deaf children to more elements of English vocabulary and grammar would improve the children's writing skills.

A second reason for creating MCE systems was to enable signers to distinguish among the various forms of English words, such as *excite/excitement, instruction/instructional,* and *handy/handiness.* In reality, ASL already had techniques for making such distinctions, but they were underutilized and not well documented. Deaf teachers had long used a combination of signs and fingerspelling and various ASL features for this purpose, but their techniques were known by only a few people. Unaware of ASL's versatility in such matters, the creators of MCE invented signs for English affixes such as *-ment, -tion, -al,* and *-ness,* and for verb tenses such as the present, past, and progressive.

A third reason for the creation of MCE was to help parents and teachers communicate with deaf children without having to learn a new grammar system. Most teachers and parents are hearing, and English is their first language. English is the primary language in most homes and schools in the United States. MCE provides a convenient vehicle for conveying English.

The original MCE systems were Signing Exact English, Signed English, Seeing Essential English, and the Linguistics of Visual English. Each of these names includes the word "English," but the systems use English structure to varying degrees. Aside from the school system in Amarillo, Texas (which uses Seeing Essential English), Signing Exact English and Signed English are the only MCE systems now used in total communication programs in the United States. Chapters 6 and 7 describe these two systems.

From English to ASL

Total communication programs showed that teaching in signs did allow for academic and linguistic growth in deaf children. While these programs were not the answer for all deaf children, the language and literacy skills of many of the children flourished with exposure to English signing.

From the beginning, some people objected to the notion of creating signs to represent English. They said that MCE was too awkward to use and that it neglected many of the principles of signing in a visual medium, which ASL exemplified. They claimed, rightly, that many teachers and parents did not use MCE the way it was meant to be used. Most people in the field used a form of MCE whose grammar conformed neither to English nor to ASL. This prevalent form of signing, called Pidgin Sign English (PSE), is viewed as a mixture of English and ASL signing. Today it is more commonly called contact signing.

In practice, contact signing rather than MCE was, and still appears to be, the most widely used form of signed communication in total communication programs. But when total communication programs were first gaining a foothold in the field, few if any of them openly endorsed contact signing. How could they? We are only now beginning to understand the social and linguistic traits of contact signing. Some total communication programs now endorse it as the preferred means of signed communication for the classroom. But twenty years ago, it carried little credibility. This left MCE as the perceived champion in total communication and, as we shall see, its subsequent scapegoat.

Resentment toward MCE soon shifted to the principles of total communication, especially in the 1980s. Cultural pride was growing in the Deaf community, and ASL was gaining recognition as one of the strongest identifying elements of Deaf culture. Why, Deaf people asked, is ASL not being used in schools to teach deaf children? The backlash began against total communication programs and MCE in particular.

Why, indeed, was ASL not used in the total communication approach? After all, the philosophy advocates the use of whatever methods teachers deem effective in communicating with their deaf students, and there is no inherent reason that ASL could not be the best form of communication for some children. (Some programs adamantly banned the instructional use of ASL, but many did not.) A simple and plausible explanation for the neglect of ASL in total communication programs is that few teachers were fluent in ASL. Moreover, there were very few instructors with the expertise and training to teach ASL to teachers. What could the teachers do? They used MCE or contact signing and spoke while they signed. To bring ASL into the education system it was necessary to show that hearing teachers could learn ASL and use it effectively in the classroom.

Along with the demand for ASL in the classroom came the call to incorporate Deaf culture into the curriculum. For many Deaf adults the Deaf community is the preferred venue for socializing and many other activities. Here, Deaf people are both the recipients and the progenitors of cultural activities. These include the arts, competitive sports and leisure activities, politics, various academic pursuits, and more. Along with ASL, activities like these comprise Deaf culture. Because most deaf children come from hearing families, it is important for educators to expose the children to Deaf cultural activities in addition to the activities associated with their parents.

The push to include ASL and Deaf culture in the education of deaf children is known as the bilingual-bicultural movement. Like total communication, the bilingual-bicultural philosophy prescribes no single approach. A total communication program could embrace the basic principles of the bilingual-bicultural movement and offer Deaf cultural experiences for students.

Because the bilingual-bicultural approach is relatively new in the field and only a handful of programs have adopted it, we don't know much about how it usually is practiced. Each program creates its own framework for using ASL as the language of instruction and teaching aspects of Deaf culture.[9] In some programs, ASL is used as the only in-the-air means of instruction and English is taught as the students' second language through reading and writing. Other programs have different approaches. The variation in programming is to be expected because bilingualism can rely on many communication strategies. Indeed, some bilingual programs include English signing and speech during English instruction. At one school, Signing Exact English is used but Deaf adults serve on the school advisory board and regularly attend school-sponsored events, and the deaf children are encouraged to learn ASL after school hours at the nearby state residential school. There is no one right way to be bilingual. The focus of these programs should be to provide a range of sound options for teaching deaf children about languages and cultures.

Putting History in Perspective

After nearly two hundred years of deaf education in the United States, certain truisms have emerged: Most deaf children will not succeed in school using only speech and audition. Deaf children receive information through signs more efficiently than through speech and audition. Signing is the dominant means of communication among Deaf adults, which tells us a lot about its value for Deaf people. Many oral deaf people become signers as teenagers. Many Deaf people sign because it is the best way for them to communicate, learn, and contribute to society.

For parents considering whether to sign with their children, the preference of most deaf adults for signing rather than speech is a message worth heeding. At the very least, we recommend that you contact the deaf education program in your school district and the nearest state school for the deaf to gain a better understanding of the available options. Find out what they consider to be the best form of signed communication and how they believe they can best educate your deaf child. Ask them for the names of Deaf adults in your area and find out how you can meet and converse with them.

NOTES

1. The signals of cued speech are designed to aid speechreading. With one hand the speaker forms handshapes that are moved about in four positions close to the face. These hand signals are not signs and should not be called a form of signed communication. In conjunction with speech they help the viewer understand all speech sounds and to distinguish between words that look similar when spoken, such as *rain* and *Wayne* or *bed* and *bet*.

2. Oral education is a method of instruction that emphasizes the development of speech, lipreading, listening skills, and written language.

3. At the time, the word "dumb" was commonly used to refer to people who did not speak and was not a derogatory term.

4. A number of the students who attended the Connecticut Asylum came from Martha's Vineyard, an island off the coast of New England. This island had a disproportionately large number of deaf people. They had an established sign language, and many of the island's natives, deaf and hearing, knew how to sign (Groce 1985). It is likely that these students introduced their signs to deaf students from the mainland. However, Stedt and Moores (1990) caution against overestimating the influence of this group because they were a very small percentage of the student body.

5. Lane 1984; Stedt and Moores 1990.

6. Lane, Hoffmeister, and Bahan 1996.

7. Moores et al. 1987.

8. Ibid.

9. For more information about bilingual / bicultural education see Mahshie 1995 and Walworth, Moores, and O'Rourke 1992.

3

A WORD ABOUT LANGUAGE

***What Parents Should Know
about Language***

- ◆ *Gestures, signs, and speech are codes used to express a
  language.*
- ◆ *ASL can be coded in gestures, signs, and nonmanual
  features.*
- ◆ *English can be coded in speech, signs, and print.*
- ◆ *To learn a language, deaf children must have access to
  the codes used to express that language.*
- ◆ *The more exposure deaf children have to a language,
  the better chance they have of acquiring it.*

IT WASN'T LONG AGO that dictionary definitions of *language*
focused almost exclusively on speech and print. Signing was viewed
as a way of communicating but not as a language. Today, this notion
has been swept away in a flood of research on the role of gestures in
signed languages and the intricate syntax that is created in a spatial
medium.

It is difficult for many hearing people to understand that speech
and language are separate concepts. You can learn to repeat phrases
clearly in Polish but that doesn't mean you can express ideas in Polish. Parrots can pronounce a few English phrases but no one says
they have learned a language. Speech does not equal language—a
revelation that was absolutely essential in convincing teachers and
parents of deaf children that signing can express language.

Similarly, we must not make the mistake of believing that all forms of hand gestures are expressions of a language. Pantomime, for example, relies on gestures, but it is not language. The ability to copy signs from American Sign Language (ASL) does not demonstrate knowledge of the language. Nim Chimpsky, a chimpanzee who was taught ASL signs, is a case in point. After many years of instruction, researchers believed that since Nim was capable of producing strings of signs, he had learned a language. Other researchers said that all Nim had learned was how to make crude approximations of ASL signs, or (in a word) to "ape" ASL. Some scientists said that even these crude approximations were just natural hand movements that apes often made in the wild.[1]

So, what is language? Language is a systematic means of communication through which ideas about the world are expressed. A language is agreed upon by a community of users who use it to communicate about ideas, actions, and processes such as thinking and dreaming.

And what is a code? A code is an agreed-upon set of symbols that represent meaning. Codes convey languages. Signing is a code. Speech is a code. The manual alphabet, Morse code, and braille are also codes.

English is a language and so is ASL, but the ways in which they are conveyed are different. English can be spoken, printed, finger-spelled, and signed as well as expressed in braille and Morse code. ASL is a manual language that does not include speech. It does, however, include facial expressions and body language, and the mouth is sometimes used to mark grammar. (This grammar can be distorted when spoken words are added.) There is no written component of ASL.

To develop expressive and receptive language abilities, all children, including your deaf child, require several conditions. First, they need access to the language. That is, they must be able to see or hear it (or in the case of deafblind people, feel it), and they need long-term exposure to at least one mature user of the language who can serve as a model. No one learns language out of thin air, although as we shall see later in this chapter the mind of an infant already has the programming necessary for learning a language.[2]

The second thing a child needs in developing language is freedom to experiment. In many ways, communicating with a deaf child is no different from communicating with a hearing child. Deaf children make the same kinds of errors in signing that hearing children make in speaking. Let's not pounce on every mistake they make. Instead, let's cherish their use of language and let them enjoy the experience, explore, and grow with their learning of the language.

The third condition for language development is the enrichment and clarification provided by gestures. Gestures are generally thought of as nonverbal communication, and they are important in that role. But they can also take on meanings and, when used in standardized ways, become signs.

THE THREE MAIN COMPONENTS OF LANGUAGE

All discussions about language at home and in a school setting revolve around one or more of its main components, which are *use, meaning,* and *form.*

Language Use

The component known as language use, also called *pragmatics,* is the set of skills having to do with conversation. In conversation language is used to serve various functions, such as asking questions, responding to what someone has said, describing something, explaining the rules of a game, giving orders, joking, and so forth. We use language to express feelings, assert values, resist control, convey abstract ideas, define words, and analyze situations.

Language use also includes the social skills involved in conversation. Perhaps it is this aspect of language use that has brought you to signing; you want to have real, in-depth conversations with your deaf child, and you want your child to have rewarding conversations with many other people. Just signing or talking is not enough. Good conversationalists know how to initiate, continue, interrupt, and end conversations. They pay attention to the topic being discussed and are able to participate in a socially acceptable manner. This is what we all do when we talk with others. We take turns, responding to what others have said, disagreeing, or (when boredom creeps up or our anxiety level becomes intolerable) diverting the discussion to a new topic. When we don't understand what someone else has said, we ask for clarification. We may even change what we have just said to make ourselves better understood. When we do this, linguists would say that we are "repairing" what we have just said.

All of these skills are used between husband and wife, parent and child, teacher and child, child and friend. Skills in language use can be achieved through any type of signing.

Language Meaning

A second component of language is meaning. The meaning of a word or sentence is its content—the information it conveys based on the conventions of usage. As young children learn language, they name things *(my dog Penny)*, describe things *(truck purple)*, talk about disappearances *(my blankie gone)* and reappearances *(more juice)*, express defiance *(No!)*, assert ownership *(my coat)*, and so on.

With inadequate exposure to language, deaf children may miss out on certain aspects of meaning. For example, the meaning of figurative language may be difficult to grasp. Words are often combined to form phrases that mean something one wouldn't expect from the meanings of the individual words. In English, when you say, *hold your horses, cut it out,* or *pile into the car,* you do so knowing that most people will understand these phrases. Just pick up any children's storybook or a reader from your child's school, and you will see how often we write nonliteral, or figurative, expressions. Children need to understand this kind of language in order to fully comprehend a story or conversation.

English also includes many words that have more than one meaning. Children's books, like those about Amelia Bedelia, often use multiple meanings for humor. In *Teach Us, Amelia Bedelia,* Amelia, mistaken for a substitute teacher, consults a list of her tasks for the day. The first is "Call the roll."

> She looked puzzled.
> "Call the roll! What roll?" she said.
> "Does anybody have a roll?"
> "I have," said Peter.
> "Do get it," said Amelia Bedelia.
> Peter opened his lunch box.
> "Here it is," he said.[3]

If children are to learn to read and write English, they must understand multiple meanings, as in *I didn't mean that* and *He is a mean boy.* Many of the words spoken and written in the primary grades are these kinds of words, called homonyms. It is easier for hearing children to learn homonyms because they hear adults use the words in different ways. This is something worth thinking about. How will the method of signing you select convey this aspect of word meaning?

Language Form

The form of a language is its grammar or syntax. Each language has its own form, although some languages share many grammatical features. Form includes word order and the rules for conveying verb tenses and plurals, among others. In English, time is expressed by changing the verb *(go, gone,* or *going)*, plurals usually by the addition of *-s* to a noun, as in *two girls, seven homes, plenty of chairs.* ASL indicates tense with time markers and can show plurality by repeating a sign (see chapter 4).

Some grammatical rules allow for the combining of ideas into parts of a complex sentence so that people can say or sign things like *The boy is running and the girl is jumping.* Some rules apply to clauses that describe someone or something: *The teacher who was sick could not come to the meeting.* ASL, too, has rules for the complex embedding of ideas, but they differ from those of English.

LANGUAGE LEARNING

Whatever type of signing you choose, you will want your child to learn a language that is rich enough to serve as a base for learning about other things, such as a second language or reading and writing. Many factors influence children's development of a language base. These factors are of special interest to parents of deaf children because these children may be starting on the road to the acquisition of language a little bit later than hearing children. Parents can minimize the delay by using a communication mode that is accessible to their deaf child. This is a very good reason for parents to learn to sign when their child is young, preferably as soon as they discover that the child is deaf.

How We Learn a Language

We learn both our vocabulary and our grammar from what we hear and see. The key to learning vocabulary is making the connection between the articulation of a word or sign and the concept to which it refers. For most people, this connection is made through communicating with others and through reading. If we never see or hear a word used, that word never becomes a part of our vocabulary.

Learning grammar is a bit different. We don't have to hear or see a sentence before being able to use it. In fact, almost every sentence we speak or sign, including the one you are reading now, is a new one. We are constantly creating new sentences with our old (and new) vocabulary. We are all born with something that helps us to learn a language, just as we are born with something that helps us learn to walk and run, to crawl and climb. Linguists call it a mental grammar, a kind of "recipe or program that can build an unlimited set of sentences out of a finite set of words."[4] All an infant needs to get this program running is to see or hear other people using a language—any language!

The key to language learning is early exposure. We need some input before we can get rolling. And the input can take the form of signs or speech. Deaf children of Deaf parents learn a signed language in the same way that hearing children of hearing parents learn a spoken language. Indeed, the process of producing language may start earlier in deaf children because infants gain control over the muscles in their arms and hands well before they can control the mouth muscles required for speaking. Children often can sign before they can speak.

Hearing or watching others use a language helps a child learn how to put words in order so that they make sense. Or more to the point, the child learns which category follows which category. In English we learn that the adjective precedes the noun, as in *the humongous appetite* and *the green car.* In French the adjective follows the noun, as in *l'appétit grand* and *l'automobile verte.* In American Sign Language both orders are acceptable.

The knowledge of how words can be ordered is acquired at a rapid pace during the first few years of life. By the time children are five years old, they have acquired most of the grammar associated with the language they are learning. This is true of hearing children learning a spoken language and deaf children learning a signed language. Deaf children parallel hearing children not only in their manner and rate of learning a language but also in the types of mistakes they make.

Two further points about language acquisition are worth mentioning. First, the longer children wait to learn a language the harder it becomes to do so. Scientists think that the critical period for acquiring fluency in a language lasts until a child is about twelve years old. After this period, the child's growth in language learning tapers off dramatically. Second, fluency in one language can help a child learn some aspects of another language. This fact is used by some to argue for the teaching of ASL as a first language, to be followed by instruction in English after the child has attained fluency in ASL.

To sum up, here is what we know about what deaf children need to learn a language effectively:

- ◆ They need access to a language, which for many deaf children means a language in signs.
- ◆ They need to be exposed to a language as early in life as possible.
- ◆ They need to observe signers who can serve as proficient language role models.

Which Language Should Be Learned First?

Will the type of signing your child uses in the beginning influence which language or languages the child can learn most easily later? Yes. If you want your child to become fluent in ASL, then he or she should be exposed early to proficient ASL signing used in a variety of different situations. This exposure might be arranged when the child is just an infant or preschooler, or it might come when the child is already in school, depending on the goals you have set for the child.

Similarly, if you want your deaf child to learn English, then early exposure to English is critical. Because English is coded in various ways, your child can experience English in the form of signs, speech, speechreading, print, and through hearing with the use of assistive listening devices. Your job is to make sure that this occurs. When speech, speechreading, and hearing are not enough, then proficient English signing must be modeled.

If children learn one language can they learn another? Absolutely. Many deaf people are proficient users of both ASL and English.

Hearing children of deaf parents often learn to sign ASL before they learn to speak English; and there is no evidence that their signing skills hinder their learning to speak. On the contrary, there is evidence that children use their knowledge of one language to learn a second language.

Nevertheless, learning a second language may not be simple. If a deaf child already knows English, there is little doubt that he or she will be able to learn ASL. This is because deaf children seldom if ever have any difficulty in learning ASL. (One exception is deaf children who do not acquire proficiency in any language by the age of twelve. Such children may still learn to sign ASL but likely not as fluently as children who learn it at an early age or who master English and then learn ASL.) Whether their parents use it or not, most deaf children can learn ASL simply by spending time with deaf friends who use it. This is one of the reasons why some teachers think that ASL should be taught first. It is easy for deaf children to learn and therefore gets them communicating quickly.

But being able to sign ASL does not guarantee that deaf children will acquire a strong command of English. Many deaf children of deaf parents who have learned ASL as infants have significant weaknesses in their English skills even after twelve years of schooling in it. So is it better for deaf children to learn English signing at home because they can always pick up ASL from their deaf friends? To answer this with an absolute yes or no would be simplistic. Many factors come into play when a deaf child tries to learn English; for example, the parents' ability to learn a new mode of communication. Some professionals say that parents find ASL more difficult to learn than English signing and that parent-child communication in ASL tends to be more awkward as a result. Others argue that English signing is the more difficult choice because some children have more trouble understanding it. Even for parents, they point out, ASL may be the most comfortable form of signing once they learn it.

The debate rages on. We can't predict with certainty what will work for a particular child or a particular parent. We do know, however, that for a child to learn any language, the language must be comprehensible to the child.

OPTIMIZING LANGUAGE LEARNING

A primary goal for you as a parent is to optimize the language environment of your deaf child, especially if your child attends a public school. One way to begin is to think about how many other people are available for your child to communicate with. Maybe it's just you and the teacher. Maybe other family members and neighbors have been willing to learn to sign. Maybe all the students in the school are learning to sign, too. Compared with their hearing peers, deaf children usually have a limited number of people with whom they can communicate.

Think about what you can do to expand your child's opportunities for communication. You can enroll the child in community activities that involve other deaf children, buy signed stories on videotapes and CD-ROMs, invite the child's friends over, hire baby-sitters who can sign, link up with other parents of deaf children and ask them for ideas. Every opportunity to communicate helps your child to develop better language skills.

As your child gets older, she will want to have deep conversations about things that truly interest her. Typically, young adolescent girls are also very curious about dating, hairstyles, and how to shave their legs. They want to talk with friends (not so much with Mom and Dad) about the changes in their bodies and their lives. Teenagers lucky enough to have the language they need can carry on these types of conversations with their school friends.

Remember when we talked earlier about conversational skills? Developing language ability through conversation—and we should add, not through drills or work sheets—is essential for deaf children. Spend time talking to your child. Look up vocabulary needed in your conversations—the signs you learn today surely will be needed tomorrow. Can you learn five new signs a day? Can you write down a word that was not in your sign dictionary and remember to ask a teacher or deaf adult how to sign it?

Everyone in your deaf child's world needs to make the effort to sign with the child. Focus on topics of genuine interest to the child, as you would with any son or daughter. Ask open questions: *Why did you make that car go to the bridge? Why do you want to go back to school tonight?* Engage the child in problem solving around the house or in school. Encourage the child to consider consequences: *I'll let you watch TV for thirty minutes, but when will you do your homework and practice your dancing?* Always remember that deaf children acquire language by seeing it used and using it themselves.

The language in your child's life must be understandable. Some deaf children can get along without signing because they comprehend speech through what they are able to hear and see on the lips. But spoken language is not comprehensible to most deaf children—which is why you have decided to sign to yours. If your child understands some basic spoken messages, perhaps you are motivated to sign because you want to converse as you would with any child about much more involved topics.

Your ultimate language goal is that your deaf child learn to understand and use the adult form of a language. If one of your aims in signing is to give your child this kind of experience, then you must be prepared to learn the chosen type of signing thoroughly and use it consistently at an adult level.

Of course, signing the adult form of a language is not something you would do all the time with very young children and infants. Children learn adult language skills through successive approximations. When your child can sign CUP, you might go out and buy colored cups. When your child can ask for the pink cup, start offering a choice between a cup and a glass. Use plastic, metal, and paper cups and plates, and challenge your child to request the one he or she wants to use. Apply this principle whenever you can in conversations with your deaf child. The family of one deaf girl had a spoon that had been bent for a child with a hand grasp problem. Because that spoon had a funny shape, it was a kitchen favorite, and the deaf girl learned to ask for *the crooked spoon, not the regular kind.* Get the idea? And it's the same with phrases. Once your child can ask for her shoes, model the phrase *a pair of shoes,* then *a piece of cake, the bottle of ketchup,* and so forth.

While you are doing what you can do to spur on language development, remember that language goals are an important part of deaf children's education. Almost every deaf child has a language goal written in his or her Individualized Family Service Plan or Individualized Educational Plan (see chapter 9), because language learning is one of the main needs of a deaf child. If parents are to take an active role in their deaf children's education, they must be involved in the children's learning of language.

Language acquisition begins in the home and community, and it is your job to see that it comes to your child from many sources, in a form the child can absorb. (Language in, language out!) You need not be slim and tall or an actor or athlete to be a language role model for your deaf child. Once you've made a decision about signing, run with it. Don't hesitate too long—deaf children cannot be put on hold while we figure out how best to reach them.

NOTES

1. Pinker 1994.

2. Children learn the quality of language to which they are exposed. If they see or hear slang, incorrect grammar, or a unique vocabulary, they will learn those words and forms of expression. If they see or hear correct grammar, figurative expressions (e.g., *I have millions of things to do!*), and so forth, they will learn them.

3. Peggy Parish, *Teach Us, Amelia Bedelia* (New York: Greenwillow Books, 1977).

4. Pinker 1994, 22.

4

AMERICAN SIGN LANGUAGE

Why Parents May Want
to Learn ASL

- *ASL is the language of the Deaf community.*
- *ASL can readily be acquired by deaf children who interact with other ASL users.*
- *ASL evolved as a language for social interactions.*
- *Fluent users of ASL have greater access to Deaf culture.*
- *ASL can provide deaf children with a first language base that helps them communicate and learn during the early school years.*
- *Signing skills associated with ASL can be transferred to English signing.*
- *Deaf children's comprehension of concepts may be better when signed in ASL.*
- *ASL classes are offered in many communities in colleges and universities and adult education programs.*
- *Many books and videos are available to help parents and deaf children learn ASL.*
- *Television programs are produced by Deaf people and signed in ASL.*

TELEVISION MARKED THE COMING OF AGE for American Sign Language. A few years ago newscaster Peter Jennings mentioned in passing that personnel at the American Embassy in Moscow, which was heavily bugged, might use American Sign Language for secret conversations. He made no attempt to explain the term, evidently assuming that everyone had heard of ASL. When a TV anchor makes such an assumption on national news, ASL truly has made it into the living rooms of our nation.

There are differences of opinion among professionals and signers as to the proper definition of ASL, which we will not attempt to resolve in this book. Interested readers should consult more technical discussions of ASL.[1] What we would like to do is provide you with a working definition of ASL and point out some of its unique linguistic features.

WHAT IS ASL?

American Sign Language, or ASL as it is commonly called, is the sign language used in the American Deaf community. This definition may seem simplistic but it is an apt description for most purposes. Consider the question "What is English?" One response would be, "It is the language spoken by the majority of people in the United States, Canada, Australia, and the British Isles." For the geographically disinclined a more straightforward answer might be, "It's what we speak." Many of us couldn't define English in terms of its history or its classification as a Germanic language, and why would we want to? To say that American Sign Language is the language deaf people sign when communicating with one another defines it for practical purposes.

This definition does not refer to the complex grammar and extensive vocabulary of ASL. But all languages are complex and contain sufficient vocabulary to meet the communication needs of the populations that use them. Everything that can be said in English can be translated into ASL. As you will see, the translation is not a simple matter of substituting a sign for a word; it is a complicated process whose accuracy depends on the translator's knowledge of the two languages and the cultures associated with them.

And what do we know about ASL? For starters, ASL is the most widely researched sign language in the world. ASL research is the springboard and model for studies of many other sign languages. Yet

ASL has not always been recognized as a language. For a long time, it was mistakenly thought to consist of signs that were haphazardly strung together without the benefit of any grammatical features. The consensus during this period was that ASL was "broken English"—that it used ungrammatical English as its basis of organization. With this understanding, who could possibly advocate its use in the classroom?

But that picture of ASL is wrong. Much of our past misunderstanding of ASL stemmed from the natural tendency to substitute one word for one sign and then examine the resulting string of words. When you first saw someone sign, didn't you wonder what a particular hand movement meant? Perhaps you were told that the meaning of a particular sign was BOY. You mimicked the hand movement and there it was, your first sign. Before long you learned a few more signs. Your first impression of signing had been shaped—you assumed each sign had an English word equivalent. If you applied your new learning to a string of ASL signs, you ended up with a sentence that may have made sense but didn't sound right in English. Of course it didn't—because the ordering of signs in ASL does not correspond to the ordering of words in English. This difference can be seen in the following examples:

English: The boy jumped over the fence.
ASL: FENCE BOY JUMP-OVER.

English: The woman with the black coat is twenty-nine years old.
ASL: WOMAN THERE COAT BLACK AGE TWENTY-NINE.

Furthermore, the process of writing down ASL signs by using English word equivalents, called glosses, is not an accurate way of documenting ASL. It leaves out too much information that can be seen in the signing but cannot be expressed adequately in print. The lackadaisical movement of the sign WORK in a story about a lazy person cannot be matched with a single English word. A single sign showing a car sideswiping another car cannot be glossed by a single English word. Nevertheless, it was through the written documentation of ASL that linguists succeeded in raising the status of the language by showing that its grammar is unique, systematic, and not derived from English.

A comparison of ASL and English was necessary to demonstrate that ASL has a unique grammar. This unexpectedly led some people to postulate a rule of thumb for identifying ASL: If the order of signs does not follow English grammar, then the signing is ASL. This simplistic criterion does no justice to the complexity of ASL. In reality, ASL has a range of grammatical forms, some of which are similar to English. The ASL sentence HE HIT PETER is exactly the same in English, for example. But overall, the visual-spatial nature of signing has created a grammar that is unique and in some sense unparalleled in a spoken language.

Understanding that ASL has many unique grammatical features is an important step toward appreciating its value in deaf children's development of communication skills. Parents who select ASL as a language to use with their deaf children should be prepared to learn a variety of ways to sign the same idea. They should expect their deaf children to acquire a sophisticated grasp of ASL signs and structures as their experience with ASL increases. Parents should not be discouraged if they fail to keep pace with their children's knowledge of ASL. The children, after all, could be exposed to a lot more ASL, at school and in the company of deaf friends.

The complexity of ASL signing is often overlooked by nonsigners and beginning signers. People may think ASL is easy when they see someone signing a few simple sentences that contain pantomimed representations. But ASL is not pantomime. On the contrary, the thoughts that signs portray and the facial expressions and body movements that accompany these signs distinguish ASL as a language. ASL signs are used not only to represent objects and concepts but to create images in the space around the signer that then influence the formation and grammar of the signs that follow.

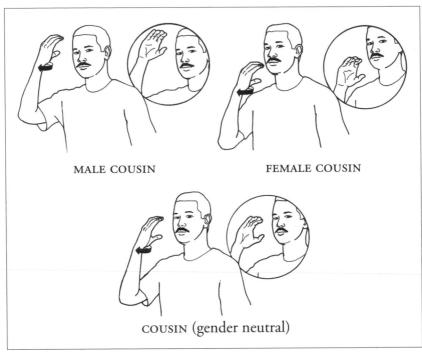

MALE COUSIN   FEMALE COUSIN

COUSIN (gender neutral)

FIGURE 5. The place where a sign is made on the face can indicate gender.

Images in space? Consider this example. A signer is describing a day in which she spent considerable time going back and forth between her home and school. At the beginning of the story she signs MY HOUSE, forming HOUSE on the right side of her body, then MY SCHOOL, forming SCHOOL to the left. She then describes what she did at home and at school by signing to the right and left, respectively. For example, *After my test, I chatted with friends* is signed to her left; *I read a magazine and watched some TV,* to the right. The person watching her sign knows that she chatted with friends at school and watched TV at home. This characteristic of signing, which is a sophisticated use of the signing space, cannot be duplicated in a spoken language.

The body has a critical role in the expression of signs. This can be seen in the signs pertaining to maleness, which typically are formed at the forehead, and those pertaining to femaleness, typically formed at the side of the chin. If the sign COUSIN is made at the forehead, it refers to a *male cousin*. The same sign made at the chin refers to a *female cousin*. And how, you may ask, do we sign *cousin* with no reference to gender? The answer, as illustrated in figure 5, is to sign it midway between the forehead and chin.

Another example of the body's role in signing can be seen in the location of signs that refer to emotions. Many of these are made near the heart or stomach, for example, FEEL, DISGUSTED, LOVE, INSPIRED, DEPRESSED, ENJOY, HAPPY, and SORRY.

While we cannot provide a thorough description of ASL grammar in this text, some additional features are worth noting. Awareness of them will help parents see how ASL compares with other forms of signed communication.

THE STRUCTURE OF ASL

A language made of signs in space will be structured differently from spoken languages. This is because the rules governing what the hands can do in space are different from those that dictate how sounds can be put together. Still, most languages share some characteristics with other languages, and ASL is no exception. In the following pages we highlight some of the important characteristics of ASL.

Context

Context, important in any language, is especially so in ASL. The sentence *What a beautiful throw* means little without knowledge of the context in which it is said. What was thrown? A basketball, a Frisbee, or a crumpled-up piece of paper? The sign THROW is made

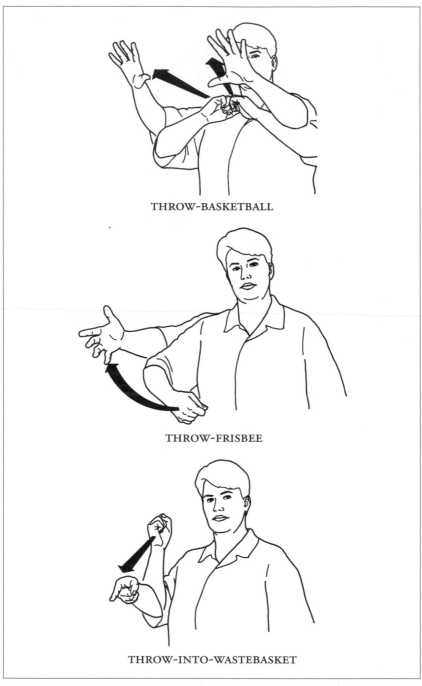

THROW-BASKETBALL

THROW-FRISBEE

THROW-INTO-WASTEBASKET

FIGURE 6. How a sign is made provides context for understanding the intended meaning of the sign.

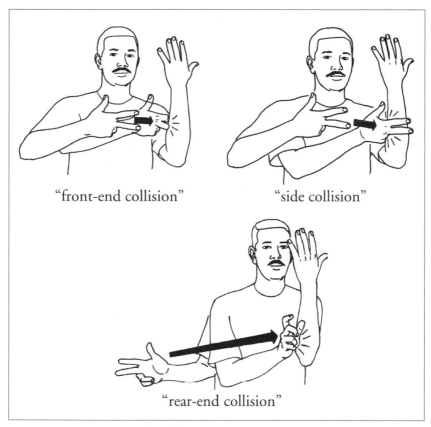

"front-end collision"   "side collision"

"rear-end collision"

FIGURE 7. The point of impact of two objects is shown by where the hands meet.

differently in each of these circumstances (see figure 6). The hands mimic the act of throwing each object.

Similarly, the way *running water* is signed depends on where the water is coming from. Water running from the nose and water running from the tap are signed differently. The place where the water runs from determines where the sign is made. Likewise, the sentence *A car hit a tree* varies depending on whether the front, side, or rear end of the car hit the tree (see figure 7).

ASL relies on conversational context to distinguish between word forms with the same root, such as some nouns and adjectives.

INSTRUCTION and INSTRUCTIONAL are signed the same way; so are VICTORY and VICTORIOUS. The signer must rely on the context of the conversation to indicate the exact meanings of such signs. Other distinctions between similar forms are indicated by movement. This is true for nouns and verbs that have identical signs. In these noun-verb pairs the verb is signed with a single movement while the noun is signed with a double movement. Some examples are AIRPLANE and FLY, CHAIR and SIT, KNOWLEDGE and KNOW (see figure 8).

Incorporation

The gestural and spatial qualities of ASL allow for more than one concept to be embedded in a sign. This process is called *incorporation.* One example of how this is accomplished is number incorporation. The sign WEEK is made with the 1 handshape sliding across the palm. If a 3 handshape is used to make the sign then the meaning is *three weeks.* Similarly, the sign NEXT-YEAR can be changed to IN-TWO-YEARS simply by changing from a 1 handshape to a 2 handshape when making the sign NEXT-YEAR. There are a handful of signs that follow a similar principle for incorporating negation into a sign. This is usually done by adding another movement to a sign. For example, the sign KNOW, made by touching the forehead with the fingertips, changes to DON'T-KNOW by flicking the hand outward. In the same manner, WANT becomes DON'T-WANT.

Another form of incorporation allows the subject and object of a sentence to be conveyed through the movement of the sign. For example, starting the sign GIVE near the body and moving outward conveys the meaning *I give you,* while starting the sign away from the body and moving it toward the chest conveys the meaning *you give me.*

Time

In English, varying verb forms such as *tell, told,* and *will tell* indicate whether something takes place in the present, past, or future.

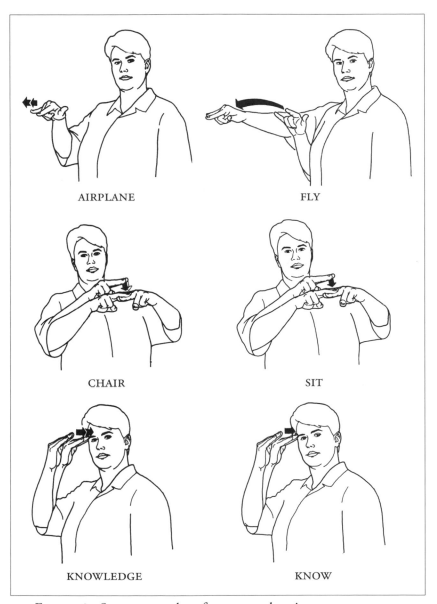

AIRPLANE

FLY

CHAIR

SIT

KNOWLEDGE

KNOW

FIGURE 8. Some examples of noun–verb pairs.

In ASL, time markers are signed at the beginning of a sentence to indicate tense. For example:

> English: I went to the house yesterday.
> ASL: YESTERDAY, ME HOUSE GO.

Once a time marker has been used, it is understood that the utterances that follow will have the tense indicated by the marker. The tense changes only when a new time marker is used, or when the context of the conversation changes, as in the following sentences:

> English: I have a meeting at school tomorrow. Are
> you hungry? Would you like to go out for
> a pizza?
> ASL: TOMORROW, SCHOOL MEETING ME GO.
> YOU HUNGRY? YOU WANT GO PIZZA?

The phrase YOU HUNGRY? introduces a new conversational context, which signals a return to the present tense.

Signs and Space

The signing space is the space in front of the body where the hands can move about freely without effort. It extends slightly off to the sides of the body and from waist level to just above the head. There is nothing to stop a signer from signing outside of this range when the message calls for it or the signer wishes to indulge in exaggerated signing. But nearly all signing takes place within a signing space that is comfortable to the signer.

Facial Expressions and Other Nonmanual Signals

Facial expressions and other nonmanual signals such as shoulder movement and eye gaze are obvious when one watches a person sign ASL. Yet until recently, flat and inexpressive signing was the norm among hearing people who signed. This is changing as today ASL is seldom taught without nonmanual signals. These signals are also called *facial grammar.*

In spoken language vocal intonations play an important role in determining the meanings of words and phrases. We can use the same words in the same order to say different things, depending on intonation. *The cows are in the field* can be expressed as a question, as a surprised discovery, a warning, and so forth. Nonmanual signals in ASL give users the same flexibility.

Proficient ASL signers are aware of the many facial expressions and body movements that inject meaning into a phrase. Raising the eyebrows and tilting the head forward signals a yes/no question. Turning the body to one side shows that a signer is referring to a concept that has been "placed" there (recall the example of a signer who placed the images of a school and a house in the signing space). Pursed lips and furrowed brows add intensity to signs, changing the meaning of *large* to *enormous, distant* to *remote,* and so forth.

Many people who learned to sign when they were adults are reluctant to accompany their signing with appropriate facial expressions and body movements. Years of speaking and a social taboo on physical expressiveness in conversation may explain this. Their reluctance is at odds with the fact that many physical expressions are part of everyday speech. For example, consider the way we shrug our shoulders, turn the palms up, and make a face when we say "I don't know." ASL should feel just as natural once social inhibitions about signing and using your body to communicate are removed.

WHAT ASL IS NOT

Having illustrated some features of ASL in print, we must now issue a disclaimer: There is no written form of ASL. And ASL can't be spoken. It can only be signed. What we have done here is write down transcriptions (glosses) of ASL. Glosses help us understand ASL but they are not the written form of ASL.

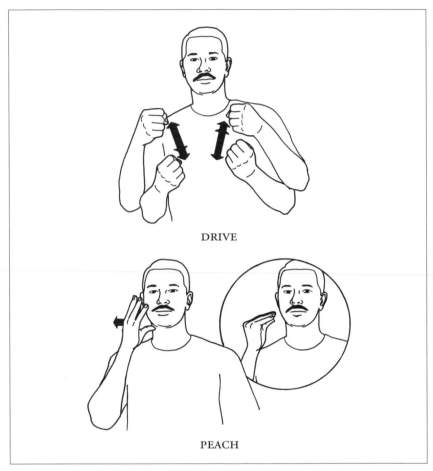

DRIVE

PEACH

FIGURE 9. Some signs are iconic (e.g., DRIVE), but most are not (e.g., PEACH).

ASL signs are not iconic, or visual, representations of the concepts being expressed. Only a handful of signs are pantomimed in the sense that their meaning can be guessed by most people who do not know how to sign. When we see the signs BABY or HAIR, we immediately recognize a relationship with the things they represent. The signs MEMBER and WRONG, on the other hand, evoke no such recognition. Figure 9 illustrates one sign that is pantomimed or iconic (DRIVE) and another that is not (PEACH). The number of iconic signs is minuscule in relation to the number of signs in the language. And the iconic signs are bound by the same rules that regulate other ASL signs.

It is often said that signers "draw pictures in the air." But ASL sentences are not pictorial. Signers create images in the air, but the meanings of these images must be learned. Thus, only in the figurative sense is signing pictorial. To see the pictures you must first know the code—you must know not only the vocabulary of ASL but also its grammar, the rules for stringing signs together. Only then will you be able to unlock the meaning of signs.

ASL is not universal. Most countries have their own sign language. There is an invented form of signed communication called Gestuno that is used at international meetings of Deaf people,[2] but it has not found its way into the signing of Deaf adults outside international sports events, conferences, and meetings. We are frequently asked by parents whether learning ASL will enable their children to talk to Deaf people from other countries. The answer is no and yes. ASL signs are different from the signs used in other countries, such as Danish Sign Language and Australian Sign Language. Even signs used for common concepts such as *girl* and *boy* and for numbers and colors are distinct from one sign language to another. Some sign languages, however, may share a large body of common signs because of mingling or borrowing in the course of their development. French Sign Language and ASL have many similar signs because of historical events that linked French Sign Language with the education of deaf children in the United States almost two centuries ago.

With some effort, fluent signers are often able to converse with people who know a different sign language. They accomplish this by seeking out a few signs shared by the two languages and combining them with gestures and pantomime. But what they are using is not ASL. There is no single language of signs that is readily understood by most Deaf people in the world.

THE BENEFITS OF ASL AS A LANGUAGE CHOICE

There are a number of reasons why parents may want their children to learn ASL. A primary reason is that many deaf children learn ASL more easily than any other form of signed communication, provided they are exposed to it. Because of its ease of acquisition, ASL gives deaf children a language base that enables them to communicate with other ASL signers at an early age. The children can also apply the language skills associated with ASL to the learning of English as a second language, even though the grammar of the two languages is very different. Of course, for deaf children in a bilingual-bicultural school program, learning ASL and English is essential to academic success.

Access to a Community

While the foregoing reasons for learning ASL may be compelling, there are others. In particular, the social and cultural dimensions of signing are worth noting. ASL provides access to the Deaf community and Deaf culture. Most Deaf people in the Deaf community use ASL when talking to one another—it is their preferred means of signing and for many it is the only means. If a deaf person wishes to experience the full benefits of interacting in the Deaf community, knowledge of ASL is essential.

Hand in hand with greater access to social interactions comes access to the values of the Deaf community and awareness of commonalities among Deaf people. Deaf people place a premium on face-to-face interactions with one another, and they appreciate their Deaf clubs for this reason.

From the Deaf clubs there have emerged a variety of organizations of Deaf people that aim to fulfill the social, emotional, and physical needs of their memberships. The American Athletic Association of the Deaf (AAAD) and its many member groups sponsor sports events in slo-pitch, basketball, tennis, and other sports that are specifically for deaf competitors. The AAAD selects and trains athletes to compete in the World Games for the Deaf, which provides athletes, sports directors, and fans with further immersion in the world of Deaf people. The National Association of the Deaf and its state affiliates sponsor social events such as dances, banquets, and casino nights as well as providing workshops on education, careers, finances, and other matters. The World Recreation Association of the Deaf sponsors leisure activities such as camping trips in national parks, Caribbean cruises, and noncompetitive games at local parks and beaches. Deaf people are active in the performing arts, appearing on stage, in movies, and on television. The National Theatre of the Deaf is well known for bringing insights about Deaf people to audiences across the nation. It is not unusual to find Deaf actors portraying Deaf characters on screen and there is much protesting by the Deaf Entertainment Foundation when a hearing actor is given the role of a Deaf character. These are just a few of the organizations and activities through which Deaf people come together and participate in Deaf culture. They provide a haven for Deaf people where communication flows easily.

Greater Self-Awareness

All of these organizations are part of the larger goal of self-determination for Deaf people. Their activities are organized by Deaf people and are for Deaf people. Hearing people are welcome to participate, and spouses, children of Deaf parents, friends, and parents do join in. But the activities are aimed at the Deaf population and are conducted with a large measure of pride by Deaf people. The leaders of these organizations are, by and large, ASL users.

When people belong to a community organization or participate in events it sponsors, they have greater opportunities to assimilate the culture of that community. Self-determination—the control that Deaf people exert over their own community affairs—is part of Deaf culture.

It is not uncommon for Deaf people to spend most of their working days in environments where they are the only Deaf person.

The endless riddle of communication with hearing people hampers attempts to explore friendships. Deaf community activities help Deaf people counter the isolation experienced in their work, mainly because of the greater ease of communicating in signs.

Taking part in the Deaf community makes it easier for newcomers to assimilate the cultural traditions of the community. They learn about Deaf leaders and the history of the community. They learn about legends, beliefs, and the customs that nurture the tales of Deaf folklore. They hear about the trials and tribulations of Deaf people in the workplace. They exchange tales of their educational experiences whether they took place in a school for deaf children or a public school. In church, synagogue, mosque, or temple they watch religious sermons delivered in signs. Each of these encounters is another chance for Deaf people to gain greater awareness of themselves by understanding more about others who are just like them.

Social Identity

ASL and the social identities of the Deaf people who use it are closely intertwined. It is a language that Deaf people can call their own, whether they have learned it from Deaf parents, from Deaf friends at school, by socializing in the Deaf community, or by taking classes during their adult years. When Deaf people use ASL they are showing their affiliation with the Deaf community because there is no other community that uses ASL as the dominant language. For a deaf person who does not know ASL, learning it and using it will signal this person's acceptance of the social identity associated with ASL. Deaf children learning ASL are in the process of assuming one identifying trait of a Deaf person.

At one level, the social identity of a Deaf person transcends racial and ethnic status. An African American Deaf person and a Caucasian Deaf person employed in a large factory will very likely strike up an acquaintance because they both sign. They are drawn together by the need to communicate. They identify with one another as Deaf people because of their experiences with hearing loss and their shared language. But Deaf people of similar ethnicity do come together too because many of them maintain some identification with their ethnic group. They have multiple social identities just as many hearing people do.

WHO USES ASL?

ASL is used in the Deaf community, in schools, churches, and homes, on videotapes, videodiscs, and television, in books, and on the World Wide Web.[3] It is one of the fastest-growing fields of second language study at the university level in the United States. Many states include ASL among the languages to fulfill the language requirement at the high school level. Even textbooks about manually coded English encourage parents and teachers to learn ASL.

Most deaf children will learn ASL at some point in their lives, either from deaf school-age peers or later when they begin to socialize in the Deaf community. Even children who attend oral schools or public schools that use only English signing sometimes pick up ASL signing skills.

At the international level, ASL enjoys some of the prestige accorded to English. Americans as a group are reluctant to learn other languages, and schooling in the United States is essentially monolingual—all English. A Dane visiting a town in Nebraska would be surprised to find storekeepers and restaurant owners conversant in Danish. But it is not unusual for Americans to travel to other countries and meet people who speak some English. Similarly, few Deaf Americans are able to converse in a sign language other than ASL. When traveling to other countries, however, they often meet Deaf people who sign a bit of ASL.

LIFE IN AN ASL FAMILY

In most families that use ASL, the parents are Deaf. If parents use ASL to communicate with one another then it is natural for them to use it with their deaf children, and with their hearing children too, for that matter. But to portray a Deaf family in this section wouldn't make much sense. It is simply not fair to say to hearing parents, "Here's how Deaf parents use ASL with their children and you can do the same thing." Although values may be similar in hearing and Deaf families, the types of communication they normally use and the communities in which they interact are too different.

One goal of this book is to show you how signing works in families much like yours. Taking into consideration all members of the family is important because communication in a family is a family affair. Your deaf children should know what you are saying to your hearing children, and your hearing children should know what you are signing to their deaf siblings.

So let's introduce you to the Randalls. The parents, Tom and Ellie, are both hearing. They have a hearing son, Max, and a deaf daughter, Brenda, who is three years younger than Max. Brenda is now six years old and enrolled in a self-contained classroom of deaf children, ages six to eight.

Ellie made the decision to use ASL in the Randall family. Brenda had been diagnosed as deaf at eighteen months of age. At that time Ellie went to talk to the teacher of a total communication program in her school district. The teacher didn't adhere to any particular kind of signing, although she had been trained in a teacher preparation program to use ASL. The school district did not have a sign language policy. This meant that the teacher was free to use whatever type of signing she chose, as long as she was meeting the communication needs of her deaf students. Ellie also talked to parents of deaf children in the program but could not decide what type of signing to use.

She had too many unanswered questions. Who used what type of signing? What would happen if she made a poor choice? Why did some people like English signing, some ASL? Why did some feel comfortable using both? So Ellie went to the state school for deaf children. The school used ASL and a modified version of Signed English for instructional purposes. She met several Deaf adults at the school and on the basis of conversations with them she decided to start off with ASL.

Ellie's first step was to enroll part-time in an interpreter preparation program. She correctly assumed that this would force her to learn ASL without interfering too much in family life. She completed the program after two years, when Brenda was five years old.

Today, Ellie considers herself proficient in ASL, although she openly admits that she can't always follow conversations between Deaf people. Her husband, Tom, has learned to sign by taking two ASL courses and practicing with Ellie. His skills are nowhere near Ellie's, and he often just fingerspells what he wants to say. He finds ASL difficult to learn but is comfortable using what he knows. Max has picked up a few signs and fingerspelling.

As a preschooler Brenda was enrolled in a parent-infant program conducted by the state school for the deaf. A teacher of deaf children gave ASL lessons to Ellie and Brenda at home once a week for a year. Because Ellie was learning to be an interpreter, she too was able to teach signs to her daughter. After one year Brenda attended a state school for the deaf, and this is where she became fluent in ASL.

The Randalls believe ASL has helped them develop a very comfortable style of communication with their deaf daughter. Their goal was to help Brenda acquire a language in which the whole family could communicate freely, and they focused on expanding her ASL vocabulary. Now they very much want Brenda to become skilled in English, and they find themselves switching occasionally to English signing. However, this has more to do with the fact that English is their first language than with any attempt to model English in signs.

They prefer to leave the task of developing Brenda's English language skills to the school. They feel that ASL has given Brenda a good start during her early school years. Brenda is alert and is able to participate in classroom conversations and talk to other deaf children easily. She is being taught English through reading and writing.

ASL has allowed the Randalls to communicate effectively with their deaf daughter. They are pleased with their decision to use ASL.

By making Brenda feel good about her communication skills in her own home, they believe they have given her a good start in her education.

A Pause for Thought about Using ASL at Home

Several issues arise when parents decide to learn ASL for use in the home. First of all, because the grammar of ASL is different from that of English, it can make communicating with a deaf child more difficult, at least during the initial phase of learning. Parents may not understand the ASL vocabulary or grammar that the child brings home from school. They may be unable to respond or to expand on what has been signed. Until they become fluent they will have trouble modeling mature grammatical forms. These problems are likely to come up even if the parents are learning ASL at the same time as the child—the deaf child attends school all day and is exposed to a lot more ASL signing than the parents.

But if there is a deaf child in the family who uses ASL, it is important that at least one parent become proficient in it. Otherwise, comfortable communication will not occur. If neither parent is comfortable communicating in the language that the deaf child uses, there may be problems when it comes time to explain, discuss, and read things to the child. No one said learning ASL would be easy for parents, but learn it they must if they have chosen that mode of communication for their child.

What can parents do? Enrolling in an ASL class is usually the first step. Parents should make sure that the instructor actually uses ASL and has an understanding of ASL grammar. This is an important point because ASL instruction is still a relatively new addition to the field of education. Many ASL instructors are new and have had little or no training to teach ASL. As a result, some classes feature sign vocabulary with only a passing mention of the complex structure of the language, which makes meaningful communication impossible.

Parents should try to learn about the way their deaf child's acquisition of the language will evolve. If the child signs MORE COOKIE, a parent may wish to model a more advanced form of this request by replying MORE COOKIE WANT YOU? OKAY. COOKIE HERE. Children who are using one- or two-sign combinations should be encouraged to expand to three- and four-sign combinations. They should also be encouraged to make fuller use of their signing space. Typically, they begin by putting all of the characters in a story in the same spot. With practice and exposure to more mature ASL signers, they eventually learn to establish specific locations for each character. Parents should know about these and many other aspects of ASL. Finding an ASL instructor who can teach them should be a high priority.

Parents who choose ASL as their home language should realize that when their child begins to learn English, the parents will need to work in partnership with school personnel. The jury is still out on the question of whether deaf children can acquire English reading and writing skills without having first acquired proficiency in signed or spoken English. Proponents of bilingual-bicultural education believe that a strong ASL base is essential to the later learning of English. A strong ASL base certainly should benefit many deaf children, but how they learn English will depend on the strategies used to expose them to it.

In a bilingual home, it is important that English and ASL not be mixed in the same utterances. Separation of languages is essential for the development of a bilingual child. This doesn't mean that only one language is to be used at all times or even most of the time. Fluent bilingual signers are able to switch from English to ASL and back again during the course of any conversation. If parents find that they are unable to use two languages effectively, they should choose one and find other people who can provide the other language to their deaf child.

Becoming Proficient in ASL

Because ASL has grammatical features that are not found in English, many parents when first exposed to ASL are confused by what appear to be irrelevant or nonsensical gestures and body movements. They may get discouraged and shy away from ASL users. This need not happen, and it won't happen if parents realize that ASL is a distinct language, unrelated to English. To become proficient in ASL takes a lot of instruction and practice.

If you live in a city that has a college or university or a continuing education program, there probably will be ASL courses available.[4] Many ASL programs now require that students take an introductory course in Deaf culture before learning to sign. The reasoning is that you will be better poised to learn the language when you understand the characteristics of the community that uses it. Other programs incorporate the study of Deaf culture into their ASL courses.

Beyond coursework, you should plan to spend a lot of time practicing and learning the intricacies of this new language. Conversing with other ASL users, preferably Deaf adults with fluent signing skills, will make it much easier for you to pick up the language.

NOTES

1. For in-depth discussions of the nature of ASL, see Fischer and Siple 1990; Klima and Bellugi 1979; Lucas 1990; Sandler 1990; Schein and Stewart 1995; Stokoe 1978; Volterra and Erting 1994; and Wilbur 1979.

2. Gestuno was initially created to overcome the communication barriers at conferences sponsored by the World Federation of the Deaf. It is now also the official sign language of the Comité International des Sports des Sourds (International Deaf Sports Association). For more information about Gestuno, see Schein and Stewart 1995.

3. For an example of signing on the World Wide Web, check out http://commtechlab.msu.edu/sites/aslweb/browser.html. This Web site was created by David Stewart, in collaboration with Dr. Carrie Heeter and her computer technicians, in the Communication Technology Laboratory at Michigan State University. It contains more than three thousand video clips of ASL signs.

4. See Schein and Stewart 1995 for a discussion of how to select sign language classes and teachers.

5

ENGLISH SIGNING

Why Parents May Want
to Learn English Signing

♦ *English is the language used in the homes of many families of deaf children.*
♦ *English signing has a written counterpart.*
♦ *English enjoys widespread use in our society. It is the language used in most books and magazines, on captioned television and video programs, on the Internet and other computer networks, in faxed messages, on the telephone with teletype devices (TTYs), and so forth.*
♦ *Parents can learn English signing without learning a new language.*

ENGLISH SIGNING is any method of coding the English language through the use of signs, fingerspelling, or both. A logical first question you may have is, Can a sound-based language like English be represented in signs, in a visual medium? Before answering this question, let's take a look at English in print—another visual medium. The printed version of English is a less-than-perfect representation, as it leaves out many aspects of speech, such as intonation, timing, facial expressions, and gestures. It can also be faulted for using various letters to represent the same sound, for example, the *c* and *k* in *cookie*, the *c* and *s* in *receive* and *sun*, and the *s* and *sh* in *sugar* and *shoe*. Printed English fails to code accurately all elements of speech, but overall, it does the job of representing English. So it is with English signing. Signs and print both are capable of expressing English visually.

THE SYSTEMS FOR SIGNING IN ENGLISH

The formal systems for signing the English language are known as manually coded English (MCE). Other terms that are synonymous with MCE are *English sign systems, contrived signs,* and *artificial sign systems.* Some forms of contact signing provide another manual representation of English but one that is less systematic and accurate than the MCE systems. MCE is a group of formal methods that were designed specifically as educational tools for the classroom.

Teachers have long felt that deaf children need to interact with English as much as possible in order to learn its complex grammar and extensive vocabulary. Many educators believe that exposure to English in day-to-day activities helps deaf children learn it. But until the 1970s there was never a formal method of coding English in signs. (Of course, fingerspelling was always an option, but in constant use it is quite awkward. The Rochester Method, which required teachers to fingerspell at all times, is no longer in use.)

A group of educators, parents, and other professionals got together at the end of the 1960s to create several systems for signing English that could assist deaf students in learning to read and write. We have chosen to concentrate on two of these systems, Signing Exact English[1] and Signed English,[2] because they are the dominant forms of MCE used in today's schools. But first we would like to discuss briefly two other MCE systems because they show how far educators were willing to go in pursuit of practical ways to sign English. They also illustrate the typically short life span of some invented sign systems.

MCE Systems That Did Not Last

Seeing Essential English and Linguistics of Visual English (LOVE) are rarely found in American school systems anymore. In fact, to the best of our knowledge LOVE is no longer used at all. Based on the use of signs to correspond to syllables in English, it was the least successful of the MCE systems.

Seeing Essential English, on the other hand, has been linked to reading proficiency.[3] But we can find no evidence that it is used today anywhere other than in Amarillo, Texas. It was invented by a deaf teacher named David Anthony, who published a dictionary and explanation of his system in 1971. In Seeing Essential English, signs are used for concepts and meaningful parts of words, such as *mo-* in the word *motor*. The number of signs used for a word roughly corresponds to the number of syllables in the word.

David Anthony and the deaf and hearing people who worked with him to develop Seeing Essential English were the inventors of the "two out of three" rule. This rule is important in Signing Exact English today. The rule is a way of determining whether to use the same sign for two or more words. It takes into account three characteristics of a word—spelling, sound, and meaning. If the words under consideration share two of these three characteristics, they are signed with the same sign. So the word *mean* would be signed in only one way even though it has multiple meanings: *You are mean, The mean temperature for June is 80 degrees,* and *I mean it!*

The rough correspondence between signs and syllables in Seeing Essential English can be seen in the following examples. The + indicates that several signs are put together to form an English word.

Speech:	He has butterflies in his stomach.
Signs:	HE HAVE+s BUTTER+FLY+s IN HIS sto+mach.
Speech:	The boys regularly are late for class.
Signs:	THE BOY+s REGULAR+ly ARE LATE FOR CLASS.
Speech:	I rode my motorcycle yesterday.
Signs:	I RIDE+d MY mot+r+cyc+le YESTER+day.
Speech:	He's running on the carpet.
Signs:	HE+s RUN+ing ON THE CARPET.

There are many reasons why LOVE and Seeing Essential English did not make a sizable dent in the education of deaf children. Chief among them is the fact that they are complex coding systems that require much time and effort to learn. Many people in the Deaf community actively decried their use with deaf children. Beyond the difficulty of learning them, a common argument against these systems was their lack of affiliation with the signs already in use in the Deaf community. Many Deaf people wondered why they should use four signs for *motorcycle* when a single ASL sign is available.

We will not pursue these arguments here. But parents should be aware of them because they are a part of the history of English signing that has brought the field of deaf education to its present point.

Signs Used in MCE Systems

Signed English and Signing Exact English (SEE) derive many of their signs from ASL, although the signs are used in English word order. In both of these systems the signs for common words such as *want, psychology, slow,* and *mathematics* are the same as the ones used in ASL. There are, however, many English words for which there are no single ASL signs, for example, the English articles *an* and *the,* names of cities, and names of cars. ASL signers create signs for new words and concepts, like *fax* and *microwave.* However, when a signer doesn't know the sign for an English word or doesn't want to use a sign, he or she will fingerspell it. MCE signers use the letters of the American Manual Alphabet when they fingerspell. Thus the codes in English signing include many of the language symbols already in use in everyday ASL.

FEATURES OF MANUALLY CODED ENGLISH

Signing takes place in a visual field. No hearing is necessary to understand signing. Deaf children have complete access to information in a visual field, as long as their eyesight is good. (Whether they understand what they see is another matter.) The fundamental aim of MCE systems is to expose deaf children to English in a medium in which they have complete access.

Table 1 compares the characteristics of the various types of signed communication that parents have available to them. The meaning of each characteristic is fully explained elsewhere in this text.

As noted earlier, many of the signs used in MCE systems are borrowed from ASL. Although not all MCE systems are alike, they are similar in many respects. One of the distinguishing features of MCE systems is that they create signs, and one way to create new signs is through *initialization.* By using initialization, signers can create new, but similar, signs for English words that represent the same concept. For example, MCE systems take the ASL sign CLASS and use an A handshape to sign ASSOCIATION, a C handshape to sign CLASS, a G handshape to sign GROUP, an S handshape to sign SOCIETY, and a T handshape to sign TEAM (see figure 10). All of these signs are made in a similar manner and differ only in the handshape of the first letter of the English word that is used to form each sign.

MCE systems use the process of initialization to a greater degree than ASL and contact signing do. MCE systems initialize the sign FOREST to distinguish it from TREE; ASL uses the movement of the hand to make the distinction (see figure 11). But ASL and MCE initialize some of the same signs, including HOTEL, GREEN, and THERAPY.

Another distinguishing feature of MCE systems is that they use a number of signed affixes to help code the various word forms found in English. The creators of the MCE systems all agreed that signs for affixes were needed. Affixes indicate verb tense and parts of speech (nouns, adjectives, etc.). Affixes such as those in the words evolution*ary,* invent*ed,* defend*ant,* electri*city,* and legisla*ture* are difficult to speechread. Only about 30 percent of all speech sounds are visible through speechreading, and to speechread affixes is particularly difficult. Moreover, deaf children are slow to acquire skills in the correct use of affixes, struggling to learn that *happy* is an adjective and *happiness* is a noun. Therefore, the creation of signs to indicate affixes

TABLE 1
Characteristics of Signed Communication

Features	ASL	Contact Signing	Signed English	Signing Exact English
Signs	ASL	ASL + some signs invented for MCE	ASL + some invented signs	ASL + more invented signs than in Signed English
"Two out of three" rule	No	No	No	Yes
ASL fingerspelling	Manual alphabet	Manual alphabet	Manual alphabet	Manual alphabet
Initialization	Yes (less than MCE systems)	Yes	Yes	Yes (more than Signed English)
Sign markers	None	Typically none (depends on user)	14	74
Grammar	ASL	English word order, with some ASL features	English	English
Use in Deaf Community	Yes	Yes	No	No

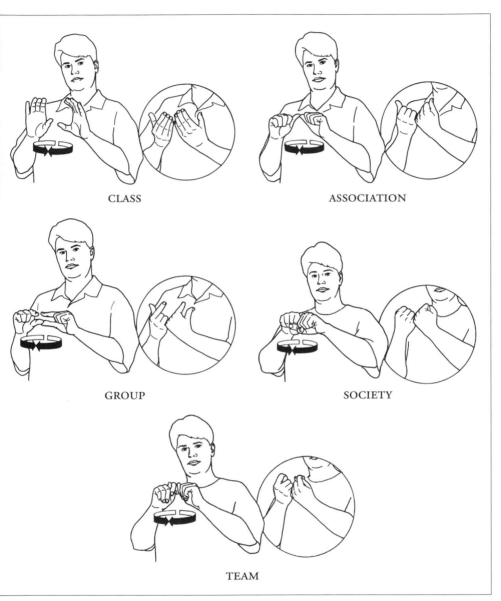

CLASS

ASSOCIATION

GROUP

SOCIETY

TEAM

FIGURE 10. Manually coded English systems create new signs through initialization.

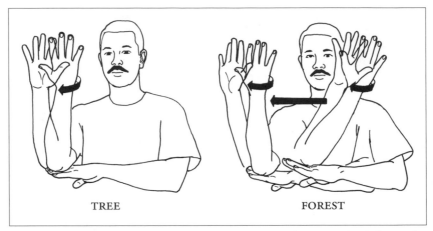

TREE   FOREST

FIGURE II. In ASL, the concept "tree" is distinguished from the concept "forest" by movement.

was thought to be critical in making English more visible and hence more understandable to deaf children. These created signs are called *sign markers.* They are used in all MCE systems to varying degrees.

When people sign manually coded English they tend to speak at the same time. It is felt that this method, called *simultaneous communication,* gives deaf children a better chance of understanding English because they have three ways of receiving it—through signs, speechreading, and listening.

The big question facing users of simultaneous communication is whether deaf children do in fact receive information through all three of these modalities. To judge by what little research is available, the answer is yes.[4] Some deaf children may not benefit from listening because they cannot hear well enough, but they can still speechread and see signs.

Some people argue that signing and speaking at the same time is inappropriate because the two modalities are incompatible. Although some deaf people disagree, the criticism is valid in the sense that both the signing and the speaking are altered when combined. Your speech rate slows down when you sign at the same time. Your signing loses some of its fluency when you try to keep up with your speech.

A visit to a classroom will show that many teachers of deaf children change the way they sign and speak in order to make it easier to use simultaneous communication. They may speak only the words that they can easily sign or fingerspell, or they may not sign all that they are saying. When this happens, the teacher no longer serves as a proficient model for deaf children learning English. On the other hand, many teachers are excellent users of simultaneous communication. The conclusion? Signing proficiently in simultaneous communication with MCE requires practice and conscientious effort.

USING MANUALLY CODED ENGLISH AT HOME

Study after study has indicated the benefits of establishing effective communication between parents and their deaf children at an early age, no matter what language or modality is used. These children are better prepared for school than other deaf children and reach higher achievement levels in their academic subjects. Therefore, if you choose to use MCE with your child, it is important that you become proficient as quickly as possible. This will help your child to master MCE early.

Finally, a word about what MCE is not. MCE is not a replacement language for ASL. We have met no advocates of MCE who are against the idea of parents learning ASL. Furthermore, MCE is a classroom- and home-based method of communication—it was never meant to be widely used in the Deaf community. ASL and MCE can coexist in the homes of deaf children.[5]

NOTES

1. Gustason, Pfetzing, and Zawolkow 1973.
2. Bornstein, Saulnier, and Hamilton 1983.
3. See Luetke-Stahlman and Milburn (1996) for more information about Seeing Essential English.
4. Bornstein 1990; Stewart 1987.
5. See Luetke-Stahlman (1996) for numerous examples.

6

SIGNING EXACT ENGLISH

Why Parents May Want to Learn
Signing Exact English

* *Signing Exact English (SEE) was invented as a communication tool for the classroom and home.*
* *SEE is suitable for parents who speak English as their first language.*
* *SEE is intended to be used simultaneously with spoken English.*
* *Parents do not have to learn a new language in order to sign in SEE.*
* *Of all the forms of manually coded English, SEE offers the most complete representation of English meaning and form.*
* *Many ASL signs are a part of the SEE vocabulary.*
* *Deaf children can learn SEE by interacting with SEE users.*
* *Many resources are available to help parents and deaf children learn SEE.*

WHEN SIGNS WERE MAKING a comeback in the classroom in the late 1960s, no materials were available to help parents and teachers sign in English (or in American Sign Language, for that matter). Many teachers were just beginning to learn about signing, and the name ASL had hardly worked its way into the consciousness of the Deaf community, let alone teachers of deaf children. People had high hopes for the expanding role of signing in the classroom, but in the beginning the situation was chaotic: Teachers used their own methods of signing in English word order and there was little uniformity in their efforts. It was the lack of a formal English signing system that convinced a group of educators and parents to develop Signing Exact English, or SEE, as it is most often called.

WHY SEE WAS DEVELOPED

The key players in the development of Signing Exact English were Gerilee Gustason, Esther Zawolkow, and the late Donna Pfetzing. Gustason, who is deaf, was teaching English to deaf children when SEE was created. She is currently a professor at San Jose State University in California, where she trains students to teach deaf children. Zawolkow, whose parents are deaf, was a certified interpreter. She now runs Modern Signs Press, which publishes SEE resource materials. Pfetzing was the mother of a deaf daughter and a classroom interpreter.[1] The work of these three people initially was centered on the development of Seeing Essential English and, to a lesser extent, Linguistics of Visual English. They eventually concluded that neither of these manually coded English systems was practical for classroom use, so they created an alternative, which they called Signing Exact English. We use the acronym SEE to refer to Signing Exact English, but it is also widely known as SEE 2, a reference to the fact that it was created after Seeing Essential English, which was called SEE 1.

Early in the development of SEE its creators approached linguists, including William Stokoe, the author of the first linguistic analysis of ASL. According to Gustason, when the linguists were asked "how to define the morphology of a signed word and the extent to which English words could and should be broken up to best represent their English morphemes," the linguists "could not really provide helpful advice." Their consensus was that the developers should "go by gut feelings." [2]

Far from feeling disheartened, the creators were spurred along in their quest to create an English sign system for the classroom for three reasons: They were dissatisfied by the low achievement levels of deaf children; there was increased evidence of the importance of language input during the first few years of a child's life; and they were concerned about the ambiguousness of speechreading alone.[3]

Of particular importance in the shaping of SEE was the research literature describing deaf children's weaknesses in English. These included the use of simple and rigid sentence structures, a small vocabulary in comparison with that of their hearing peers, difficulties in learning English words that have several different meanings, the omission of complex grammatical structures when speaking or writing, and an overall difficulty in reading. SEE was created to give deaf children visual exposure to English and to provide as much information about English words and word forms as possible. Its creators believed that SEE could also be used by parents to develop a comfortable communication link with their deaf children.[4]

Along with the SEE dictionary, the creators have published other resource materials to assist parents and teachers wishing to learn the method, including an instructor's manual and several sets of videotapes. They also have produced their dictionary on CD-ROM and videos of popular children's stories such as "Brown Bear, Brown Bear" signed in SEE.

THE TEN TENETS OF SEE

To appreciate the complexity of SEE and its possible role in the development of deaf children's language, it is helpful to know the basic tenets to which the SEE creators subscribed.

1. Acquiring good English is a tremendously difficult task for a child born deaf.
2. The most important factor in acquiring good English is an understanding of its syntax or structure.
3. Normal input must precede normal output. Aural input being blocked, visual input must be used.

4. The visual cues of speechreading are too small and ambiguous to make normal, natural language learning possible.

5. Sign language is easier to see than speechreading or fingerspelling.

6. The feeling for structure is more important than the ability to spell the word in question immediately.

7. The patterns of structure of English may easily be added to sign language.

8. It is easier to sign all parts of a sentence than to sign some and spell others.

9. Any specific sign should mean one and only one thing.

10. English should be signed as it is spoken.[5]

With these principles in hand, Gustason, Zawolkow, and Pfetzing created what has become one of the two most popular MCE systems in the United States.

WHAT IS SEE?

Signs in SEE correspond to morphemes in English words. Morphemes are the smallest units of meaning of English. A morpheme may be a basic word "from which no letters can be taken away and still leave a whole word,"[6] or it may be an affix. Words like *boy, street, world, deaf, butter, inform,* and *contain* are examples of basic words. SEE uses a single sign to represent each of them. Many of the signs for the basic words used in SEE are ASL signs. The SEE manual states that when "a sign already exists in ASL that is clear, unambiguous, and commonly translates to one English word, this sign is retained."[7] Therefore, some complex words and compound words such as *careless, understand,* and *football* are signed in SEE with a single sign.

The morphemes that are known as affixes are the smallest units of meaning in a language. We add affixes to a basic word to get complex words that have different meanings from the basic word. In SEE separate signs for affixes, called sign markers, are added to the signs for basic words. In this way SEE represents words such as *boyish, streetwise, worldly, deafness, buttery, information,* and *container.* The seventy-four sign markers used in SEE had to be invented because there are no signs for affixes in ASL. Figure 12 shows all of these markers. Sign markers are critical to the philosophy of SEE in that they are supposed to help people familiar with SEE to match each sign with a single English word. Figure 13 shows the sign markers *-s, -er, -ee,* and *-ed* added to the sign EMPLOY, which results in the signs EMPLOYS, EMPLOYER, EMPLOYEE, and EMPLOYED.

In instances where multiple affixes are added to a basic word, SEE allows the signer to drop the middle affixes if there is no resulting loss in meaning. The word *examination* is signed EXAM + -tion without the sign marker *-ine* (as in EXAM + -ine) because there is no such word as *examtion.*[8] It is expected that the person watching the signing will be able to fill in the missing part of the word. This, of course, assumes that the person is already familiar with the correct English word. For very young deaf children or for those who are just learning English, the forms of words that are signed without all their affixes have to be taught.

Where dropping an affix would create ambiguity in meaning, the affix is retained. *Developments,* for example, is signed DEVELOP + -ment + -s to distinguish it from the sign for *develops* (DEVELOP + -s).

What happens when two or more basic words are added together? Such words are called compound words. When the meanings of the basic words are not related to the meaning of the compound, a single sign is used to represent them. *Withdraw, butterfly,* and *understand* are examples of compound words that have a single sign. As shown in figure 14, compound words like *underline* and *overweight* have two signs because their meaning is related to the meanings of the basic words; that is, *underline* means to draw a line under something and *overweight* means that something weighs over what it should weigh.

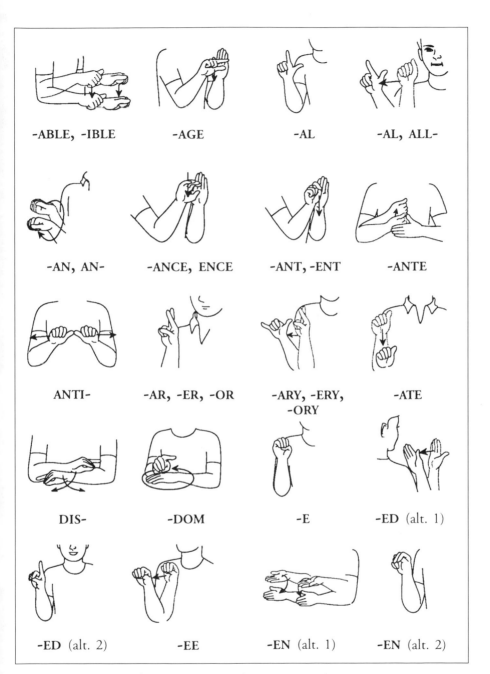

FIGURE 12. The SEE Sign Markers

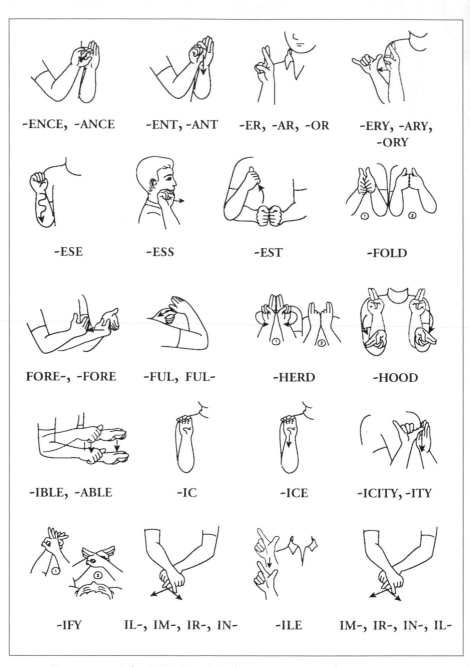

FIGURE 12. The SEE Sign Markers — *continued*

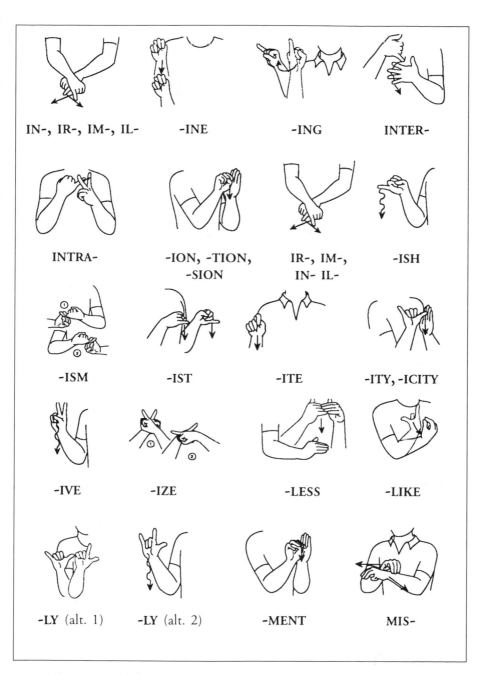

FIGURE 12. The SEE Sign Markers — *continued*

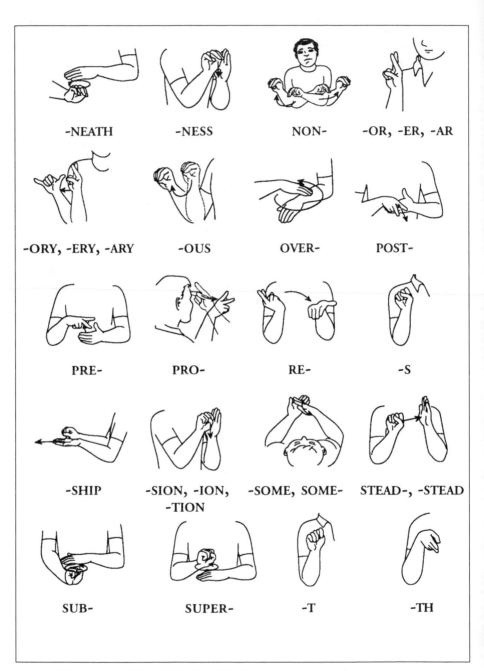

-NEATH	-NESS	NON-	-OR, -ER, -AR
-ORY, -ERY, -ARY	-OUS	OVER-	POST-
PRE-	PRO-	RE-	-S
-SHIP	-SION, -ION, -TION	-SOME, SOME-	STEAD-, -STEAD
SUB-	SUPER-	-T	-TH

FIGURE 12. The SEE Sign Markers — *continued*

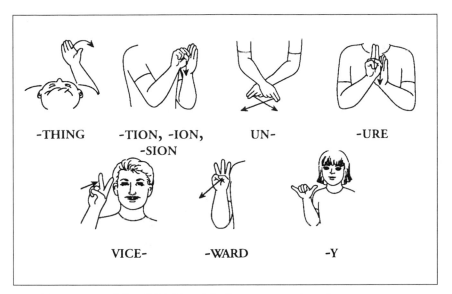

-THING   -TION, -ION, -SION   UN-   -URE

VICE-   -WARD   -Y

FIGURE 12. The SEE Sign Markers — *continued*

Let's explore how this sign-for-morpheme concept plays itself out in the following sentence, which is illustrated in figure 15.

English: It is unworkable for Corrine to be in attendance.

SEE: IT IS un+WORK+able FOR CORRINE TO BE IN ATTEND+ance.

Many English words, such as *like, run, right,* and *book,* have more than one meaning. Should there be one sign for each of the different meanings, or should they all be signed the same way? SEE uses the "two-out-of-three" rule to determine the answer case by case. As was noted earlier, the rule takes into account three qualities of a word— spelling, sound, and meaning. If any two of these qualities are the same in two words, they will have the same sign. In the sentences *You have to foot the bill* and *My foot is sore,* the sign for *foot* is the same because the spelling and sound are the same. *Whole* and *hole* have different signs because although they sound the same, they are spelled

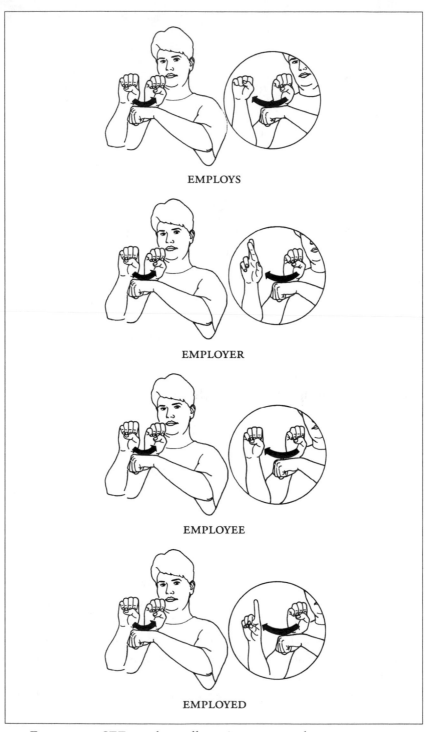

EMPLOYS

EMPLOYER

EMPLOYEE

EMPLOYED

FIGURE 13. SEE markers allow signers to make exact representations of English words.

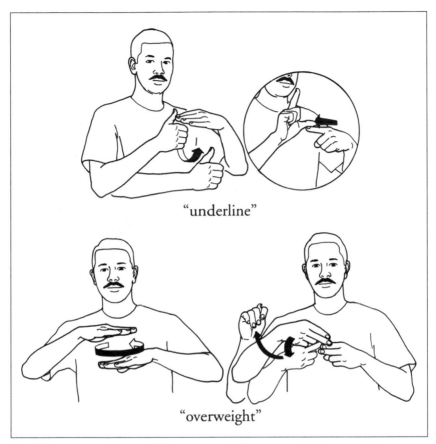

"underline"

"overweight"

FIGURE 14. Some SEE compounds are made by combining two signs.

differently and have different meanings. This rule is not used in any other popular form of signed communication.

SEE distinguishes among different words that express closely related concepts. However, ASL may use a single sign for all of them. The ASL sign MAKE is also used for some meanings of the words *manufacture, produce,* and *create.* SEE creates such words through initialization. That is, SEE uses the ASL sign but changes the base handshape to the first letter of the chosen word, for example, M, P, or C to sign MANUFACTURE, PRODUCE, and CREATE (see figure 16).

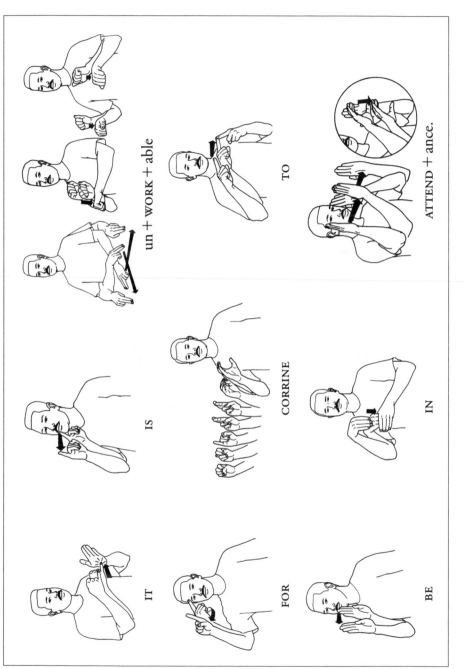

IT

IS

un + WORK + able

FOR

CORRINE

TO

BE

IN

ATTEND + ance.

FIGURE 15. The sentence, *It is unworkable for Corinne to be in attendance*, in SEE.

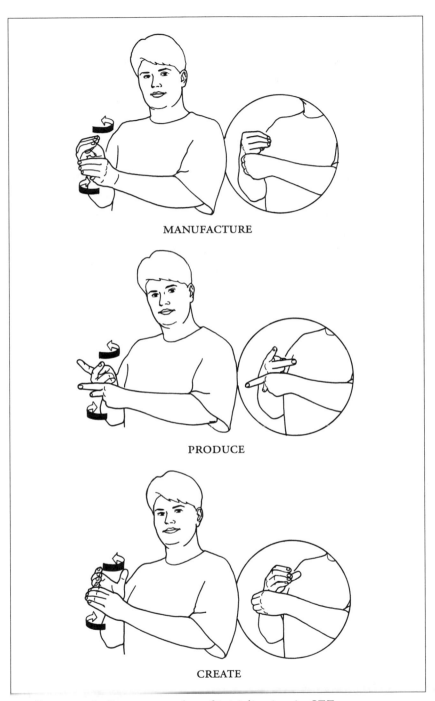

MANUFACTURE

PRODUCE

CREATE

FIGURE 16. Some examples of initialization in SEE.

Initialization is very common in SEE. Its purpose is to expand the vocabulary of deaf children who do not speechread well.

SEE AS A MODEL FOR ENGLISH

A distinguishing feature of SEE is that it never uses one sign for related words. The words *begin, beginning,* and *began* have the same base sign, but use different affixes. Furthermore, words that share the same meaning, such as *start, initiate,* and *begin,* each have their own sign. The developers of SEE believed that by signing similar words differently, children would expand their vocabularies and become better readers.

Critics say that SEE is not a natural language. We concur, in the same sense that we agree that print is not a natural language. But is SEE English? It certainly is. A more relevant question for parents would be, is it possible for an invented sign system like SEE to represent English effectively for deaf children? And can deaf children use SEE as a basis for learning to read and write English? Obviously the developers think so, and studies have shown that some deaf children do learn the complexities of English and learn to read well when they are exposed to it.[9]

The fact that SEE has enjoyed some degree of success in the field is enough of a recommendation for some parents. One mother told us that she wasn't bothered by the fact that SEE was invented because she seems to be able to do anything with SEE that can be done with spoken English or ASL. As she puts it, "I can use it to comment, describe, and explain things to my two deaf children. I use it to read to them, to complain, and to pray. They use it too, and I am satisfied with how well they are learning English." One of her daughters has the same level of English skills as her hearing peers, and the other daughter is only a year behind her peers in English and reading.

Her sentiments are echoed by other parents who use SEE. They can be a defensive lot, because some people decry any attempt to impose signing on deaf children that is not ASL. Parents who sign SEE may or may not also embrace ASL, but they continue to use SEE because it benefits them and their children.

To make SEE work as a model for English takes a serious commitment, however, as does the use of any type of signing. It is important to sign the grammar and vocabulary of English consistently. Being consistent sounds simple, but it really isn't. For a sentence such as *I have a lot of Legos,* a parent may be tempted to sign MANY MANY instead of A LOT OF because the sign MANY is ubiquitous—we often use the sign MANY with deaf children because it is so visual in showing what it represents. Some SEE signers might sign BLOCKS for convenience in place of the two signs LEGO + s (which is signed like BLOCK but initialized with L handshapes). To change your signing in either of these ways is counterproductive to the goals of SEE. It alters the child's exposure to English because he or she has to try to speechread the words *a lot of* while seeing the sign MANY. In addition, what the child learns in one situation may not be applicable in another situation if the child is learning that one word corresponds to a particular sign. A true SEE signer would sign A LOT OF if she said "a lot of."

If you decide to use SEE, you will need to follow the SEE rules, use the SEE vocabulary, sign exactly what you want to say, and continually expand your sign vocabulary. To help parents and teachers expand their SEE vocabularies and skills, Modern Signs Press, which publishes all of the SEE materials, provides workshops across the country each summer.

LIFE IN A SEE FAMILY

Betsy and Kevin have two hearing daughters and two deaf daughters. A good education and proficiency in English are their goals for their daughters—all of them! Betsy and Kevin explored ASL and all of the MCE systems and decided on SEE for two reasons. First, they wouldn't need to learn a new language to sign SEE—they felt that just learning the signs of SEE would be enough of a challenge for their family. Second, SEE provided the most complete representation of English grammar of all the available MCE systems.

Their deaf daughters, Marie and Moni, are eleven and nine years old, respectively. Betsy and Kevin are pleased with the girls' progress in English and other school subjects. Both daughters attend a suburban public school program where teachers, interpreters, and support personnel use SEE at all school activities. Thus, the girls are exposed to SEE at school and in the home.

Although Betsy and Kevin have taken only beginner-level classes in ASL, they have no difficulty in providing opportunities for Marie and Moni to become proficient ASL users. Both girls attend after-school activities at the state school for the deaf, where many children use ASL and Deaf adults are in charge of much of the programming. One of the girls is on the girls' basketball team at the state school. The girls can readily switch between English and ASL and are comfortable doing so.

Betsy and Kevin find it difficult to sign every morpheme of what they are saying when they talk fast. To overcome this problem they set goals for themselves and place a high value on signing completely. If they begin to have trouble signing every morpheme because they are excited, tired, angry, or frustrated, they simply slow down. It is important to them that Marie and Moni see grammatically accurate signed messages. That is why they place their emphasis on the English being signed, not the speed at which they sign.

Betsy and Kevin have listened to the criticisms of SEE: that it is too hard to watch, too complicated to learn, that it can strain the wrists if one signs it for too long at a time. Yet they find SEE easier to watch than ASL because English is their first language — they can predict what someone is going to sign next. This is true for the children, too, and for the neighbors and the hearing children at school.

Because they have studied the signs of SEE, Betsy and Kevin are comfortable with them. They have taken classes and often look up signs in the SEE dictionary. In fact, Betsy says, they find ASL a little more complicated: "We've studied it enough to know that very subtle sign movements can indicate important grammatical elements and that parts of the face are used in meaningful ways that are not meaningful in English. From what interpreters tell us, both methods of communication can cause wrist strain if users don't warm up, take breaks, and support their forearms."

When the family goes to a children's play or a concert and an unfamiliar interpreter is provided, the deaf girls often ask their parents or their older sisters to sign for them in the way they are used to seeing at home and school. They don't want to miss a thing.

Once when Marie was a preschooler Betsy buckled her into her car seat and warned her not to unbuckle herself. At the time the family was using an MCE system that has no sign for the affix *un-*. That system uses the sign NOT when *-un* is needed. Betsy's warning to Marie, therefore, was signed DO NOT NOT BUCKLE YOUR SEAT BELT! Marie looked terribly confused—do you want me to take it off or keep it on? she seemed to be asking. Shortly after that, the family started using SEE so that their meaning could always be conveyed accurately.

LEARNING SEE

The developers of SEE were aware of the problems that parents face when learning to sign. They noticed that there were a handful of ASL books available and almost none on the MCE systems. So they developed learning materials, including videotapes, to accompany the SEE dictionary, or the "big yellow book," as it is commonly called. The dictionary contains more than four thousand signs, all seventy-four sign markers, and instructions for learning and using SEE.

Despite the size of the SEE dictionary, you'll find it doesn't have all of the signs that you need in daily communication. Some teachers and families simply invent new signs to fill the gaps. One family felt a need to invent signs for *Cheerios* (CHEER + -o + -s), *Snickers* (the sign BAR initialized with the S handshape), and *Ernie* (the handshape E on nose) and *Bert* (the handshape B at the back of the head, representing a tuft of hair). They didn't mind inventing these signs but wished they had already been available. By the time their deaf daughter began the first grade, the parents could fingerspell the words. But when she was younger, they had fingerspelled only short words in conversation and only one or two per page in a story.

Inventing signs, did we say? We don't just off-handedly invent words in English, do we? Of course not. Many deaf people and sign language aficionados become highly agitated at the thought that each home or school might develop its own set of signs for things. The authors are in complete agreement. We recommend that when a sign is not available you first consult various ASL and MCE dictionaries. If you still can't find the sign you need, then contact a Deaf person fluent in MCE as it is used in your community. Ask if there is a local sign available that hasn't found its way into publication.

Another good source for new signs is schools for deaf children, where signs are often invented for frequently used words and expressions. The National Technical Institute for the Deaf in Rochester, New York, has developed texts and videotapes illustrating the signs for words used in various academic and professional subject areas (science, geography, and so on). Many other schools keep records of the signs they use for these purposes. Alternatively, don't discount fingerspelling as part of SEE or any other MCE system. After considering all of these options, you might consider the benefit of creating a sign that will meet your communication needs.

Notes

1. Gustason 1990.
2. Ibid., 110.
3. Gustason 1990, 108.
4. Gustason and Zawolkow 1993.
5. Gustason 1990, 112, 114–15.
6. Ibid., 116.
7. Gustason and Zawolkow 1993.
8. Gustason 1990.
9. Luetke-Stahlman 1988a, 1988b, 1996; Schick and Moeller 1992.

SIGNED ENGLISH

Why Parents May Want to Learn
Signed English

◆ *Signed English offers an approximation of correct*
  English.
◆ *Signed English has only fourteen sign markers for par-*
  ents to learn.
◆ *Parents do not have to learn a new language in order*
  to use Signed English.
◆ *Signed English is intended to be used simultaneously*
  with spoken English.
◆ *The Signed English system is designed to become more*
  like contact signing after a deaf child has demonstrated
  knowledge and use of correct English forms.
◆ *The Signed English vocabulary includes many ASL*
  signs.
◆ *Many resources are available for helping parents and*
  young deaf children learn Signed English.

THE SYSTEM of manually coded English known as Signed
English has enjoyed much popularity in schools throughout the
United States. It was developed by Harry Bornstein, Karen Saulnier,
and their colleagues in the Signed English project in the early 1970s
in Washington, D.C., for use with preschool children.[1] The system
is now used with older deaf children, too. Like all MCE systems,
Signed English is an educational tool, meant to be used in conjunction with speech as children are learning English.

The creators of Signed English developed this system because

103

they believed the available MCE systems were too complex. These other systems focused too much on the sounds and spellings of words, and they lacked age-appropriate signs for young deaf children. In addition, they didn't have many teaching materials for teachers, parents, and others.[2] In 1971 the MCE systems in use were Seeing Essential English, Signing Exact English (SEE), and the Linguistics of Visual English. Seeing Essential English and the Linguistics of Visual English have all but vanished from the classroom. Signed English has thrived, and a wide selection of books, videotapes, and other instructional materials are available for people interested in learning it.

WHAT IS SIGNED ENGLISH?

Like all MCE systems, Signed English relies on signs, sign markers, and fingerspelling to serve as "a relatively complete model of English for a child who needs to learn that language."[3] It was designed with the families of deaf children in mind, particularly families seeking a system that was easy to learn. As one of the creators said, "We wanted to develop an educational tool that was, on one hand, a reasonable approximation of spoken English and, on the other, something that could be learned and used by the largest possible group of people."[4]

The main reason for the focus on families and on a simpler system was that the developers wanted deaf children to be exposed to English in a signed form at as young an age as possible. The publication of *The Basic Preschool Dictionary* in 1972, with 980 signs, was the first attempt to accomplish that goal. Next came *The Signed English Dictionary for Preschool and Elementary Levels* with 2,200 signs, then *The Comprehensive Signed English Dictionary* with 3,100 signs.

The Signs of Signed English

What is the nature of the signing in Signed English? How does it differ from other types of signed communication? The signs in

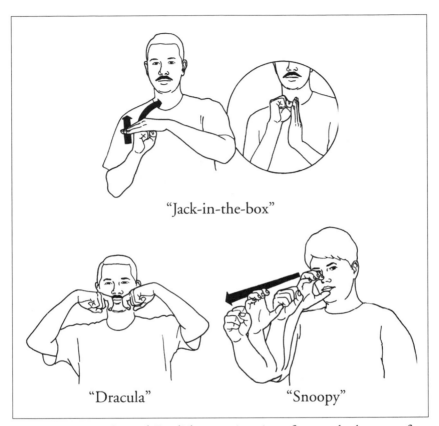

"Jack-in-the-box"

"Dracula"   "Snoopy"

FIGURE 17. Signed English contains signs for words that are often part of a child's vocabulary.

Signed English are essentially the same as those found in ASL. For example, TALE in Signed English is signed in the same manner as the ASL sign STORY, which is its synonym. To distinguish between TALE and STORY one can either say the words while signing them or fingerspell them. Speaking and fingerspelling, of course, require that the person watching can understand these modalities.

The Signed English dictionary contains some signs that are not commonly found in ASL dictionaries but often are used with young deaf children. These signs are derived from the objects to which they refer (see figure 17).

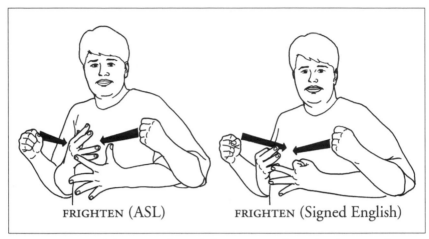

FRIGHTEN (ASL)   FRIGHTEN (Signed English)

FIGURE 18. The Signed English creators adapted ASL signs by using initialization.

Most of the exceptions to the use of ASL signs in Signed English are instances of initialization, the process of using the manual-alphabet equivalent of the first letter of the word that is being signed as the handshape for that sign. Figure 18 shows the sign FRIGHTEN as it is typically signed in ASL and as it appears in the Signed English dictionary. In Signed English both hands form the letter F.

Signed English also uses initialization to create new signs. The handshape for the ASL sign GORILLA is replaced in Signed English by K handshapes to make KING KONG. Signed English takes the ASL sign for a bird flying and substitutes P handshapes to create the sign PTERANODON, the flying dinosaur. ANTLERS, CUPID, and DESSERT are other examples of signs invented in Signed English through initialization (see figure 19).

The reason for initializing is to accommodate the need of young deaf children to acquire an extensive English vocabulary before they are able to read. Because initialized signs typically refer to only one English word, parents and teachers can use them to expand deaf children's vocabulary. But signs are created only if a sign for a word does

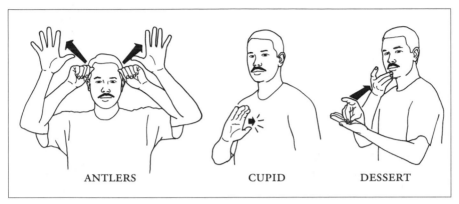

ANTLERS   CUPID   DESSERT

FIGURE 19. New signs are created in Signed English through initialization.

not already exist in ASL or if a clearer relationship to the equivalent English word is desired. Older deaf children (from second grade on) and Deaf adults are inclined to fingerspell a word for which there is no sign. It is because young deaf children have yet to acquire sufficient vocabulary and knowledge of fingerspelling that more signs have been created for them.

Sign Markers

The fourteen sign markers that represent "the most frequently used word-form changes in English" are the backbone of the Signed English system.[5] These sign markers are illustrated in figure 20. Sign markers are added to base signs to form as close an approximation as possible to English words. For example, the affix *-ly* is added to NICE to represent *nicely;* the sign marker for the superlative *-est* follows the base sign HIGH to produce *highest;* and the marker *un-* precedes REAL to produce *unreal.*

Not all sign markers in the Signed English system represent a specific set of letters. The sign marker for irregular past tense verbs is a modification of the ASL sign FINISH. It is used for the words *ran*

regular past verbs: -ed
talk*ed*, want*ed*, learned

regular plural nouns: s
bear*s*, house*s*

3rd person singular: -s
walk*s*, eat*s*, sing*s*

irregular past verbs:
(sweep RH open B, tips out, to the right)
sa*w*, hea*rd*, ble*w*

mice

irregular plural nouns:
(sign the word twice) children, sheep, mice

possessive: -'s
cat*'s*, daddy*'s*, chair*'s*

verb form: -ing
climb*ing*, play*ing*, *running*

adjective: -y
sleep*y*, sunn*y*, cloud*y*

adverb: -ly
beautiful*ly*, happ*ily*, nice*ly*

participle:
fall*en*, go*ne*, grown

comparative: -er
small*er*, fast*er*, long*er*

superlative: -est
small*est*, fast*est*, long*est*

opposite of: un-, im-, in-, etc.
(made before the sign word, as prefix)
*un*happy, *im*patient, *in*considerate

agent (person):
(sign made near the body)
teach*er*, act*or*, art*ist*

agent (thing):
(sign made away from the body)
wash*er*, dry*er*, plant*er*

FIGURE 20. The Signed English Markers

(RUN + FINISH), *went* (GO + FINISH), and other irregular verbs that do not use *-ed* to indicate the past tense.

Obviously, the fourteen sign markers do not express all English word forms. Rather, they represent the most common word-form changes in English. When signers encounter a word form for which there is no sign marker in Signed English, they can either sign the base word alone or fingerspell the entire word. For example, the words *motherhood* and *hardship* are signed as MOTHER and HARD or entirely fingerspelled.

Thus Signed English can code most of what is spoken, but not everything. The Signed English sentence depicted in figure 21 shows a complete English sentence rendered in Signed English.

> English: Happily, the judging ended early.
> Signed English: HAPPY+ly THE JUDGE+ing
>   END+ed EARLY.

Similar to SEE, Signed English requires that only one sign marker be used for any single word. The words *regretfully* and *expectedly* in Signed English thus become REGRET + -ly and EXPECT +-ly.

The rationale for including only one sign marker in a given word is that the resulting word (for example, *expectly*) is not a word in English, and so it produces no ambiguity in meaning. The only exception to this rule is when a word requires the agent marker. In these cases an additional marker can be added to the sign, so that the word *teachers,* for example, would be signed as TEACH + agent marker + -s.

The creators of Signed English were aware of the limitations of coding English with just fourteen sign markers. They argued, however, that parents and teachers were more likely to learn—and therefore to use—the smaller number of sign markers. As these sign markers represent the most frequently encountered word forms, advocates of Signed English regard this approximation of English in signs as a worthy goal. The Signed English creators believed that, as children

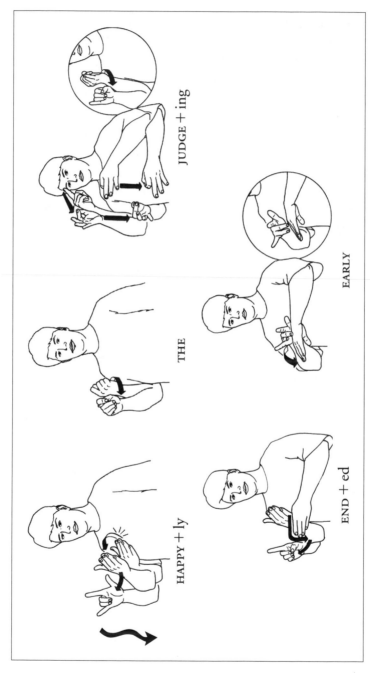

FIGURE 21. The sentence, *Happily, the judging ended early,* in Signed English.

gain a larger English vocabulary and a fuller understanding of English grammar, they will be able to infer meaning from the context and structure of the signed sentence.

SIGNED ENGLISH AS A MODEL FOR ENGLISH

The main reason parents learn to use an MCE system is to model English language word order to their deaf children. Modeling English in signs does slow down the speech rate and alter word choices. If the signing is too slow and awkward, deaf children may have difficulty understanding it, in which case the purpose of signing is defeated and parents can become discouraged. This need not happen if parents make a conscientious effort to sign well and devote the time needed to practice. We have found that when parents try to learn an MCE system well, many of them succeed.

The creators of Signed English recognized its potential for frustration. For this reason they presented it as a changeable method that becomes simplified through progressive stages. When your deaf child is young and is just beginning to acquire English language skills, it will be necessary for you to sign English as completely as possible and to use all of the sign markers. But as your child begins to show an expressive and written command of the English structures linked to the sign markers, you can begin to delete some of the markers. Further mastery of English leads to further deletion of English articles and prepositions. (The reason for deleting these affixes and words is that if deaf children already know how to use them correctly, they know where they belong in a sentence even when they are missing.) Signed English proponents believe that as deaf children become older and are able to read and write English, ASL begins to play a more significant role in their day-to-day sign communication. Deaf adolescents, if they have acquired proficiency in English, should be able to use ASL constructions to replace some English phrases.

REDUCTION IN SIGNED ENGLISH

Signed English is designed to move from a word-for-word modeling of English while a deaf child is young to a more natural type of signing that resembles ASL. The creators of Signed English recommend that this shift occur in stages, only after the child demonstrates mastery of the various elements of English. Parents can judge children's mastery of English by observing how they use it in speech, signing, reading, and writing. For instance, if a child writes proficiently in English without assistance, there is no need to continue to use a detailed form of Signed English.

The shift to less coding of English is accomplished mainly through the deletion and substitution of signs. Deletion begins with signs and sign markers whose meaning can be figured out from the rest of the sentence. Various degrees of deletion are shown in the following examples of Signed English:

English:	The girl went swimming twice last week.
Complete Signed English:	THE GIRL GO + FINISH SWIM + ing TWICE LAST WEEK.
First reduction:	THE GIRL GO SWIM + ing TWICE LAST WEEK.
Second reduction:	THE GIRL GO SWIM TWICE LAST WEEK.
Third reduction:	GIRL GO SWIM TWICE LAST-WEEK.

In the first reduction, the past-tense indicator for irregular verbs is deleted. The words *last week* indicate that the action of going swimming took place in the past, so a person who knows how to use the past tense in English can infer that GO in this sentence is correctly translated as *went*. In the second reduction, the sign marker *-ing* is removed; in the third reduction, the definite article *the* is deleted.

Knowledge of English allows a person to fill in the gaps in the reduced sentences to arrive at a grammatically correct English sentence.

But knowledge of the meaning of each sign is all one needs to understand any of these signed sentences. In other words, the meaning of each reduced sentence is intact despite the deletion of signs—only the compete representation of English has been altered. Through its progressive reductions, Signed English remains viable as a form of communication.

The third reduction illustrates another way of reducing a sentence in Signed English: substituting one sign for two or more English words. The signs LAST and WEEK are replaced by LAST-WEEK, a single ASL sign with the same meaning. Some other groups of English words that can be signed with a single ASL sign are PUT-DOWN, LOOK-UP, TURN-AROUND, IN-A-WHILE, TWO-DAYS-AGO, and CATCH-UP.

This type of substitution can be done early, when a child is learning Signed English for common nouns and popular proper names such as *French fries, hot dog, chewing gum,* and *Santa Claus.*[6] Each of these nouns has a single ASL sign. So from the beginning, children are exposed to ASL signs. The goal is for children to use and understand English correctly. By the time they reach adolescence their English literacy skills will be well developed, and it is to be expected that they will incorporate ASL characteristics into their signing.

At what point do reduced forms of Signed English cease to be Signed English? Can the third reduction of the sentence shown earlier still be called Signed English? A more accurate name at this stage would be contact signing. Indeed, contact signing is the ultimate goal of Signed English users as they progressively reduce the amount of English that is represented in their signing. The developers of Signed English view contact signing as the system of choice for the teachers and parents of deaf adolescents. Contact signing uses ASL and many of its signing features; in fact, it is so similar to ASL that some people think they are the same. Contact signing is said to be easier for hearing people to use because it follows English word order for the most part. The characteristics of contact signing are described in the next chapter.

The creators of the Signed English system advocate that deaf children begin with Signed English and move toward ASL signing as they get older. In this way the children develop the English skills necessary for academic success, and they are able to communicate in the Deaf community. Another benefit is that the parent or teacher, in changing from Signed English to contact signing, moves from the role of English modeler to that of communicator. The deaf child and the parent or teacher begin to communicate in a manner that is comfortable for both of them.[7]

At all stages in this transition, it is important that your deaf child's ability to express English form and meaning be monitored carefully. Only when there is clear evidence that he or she understands certain English forms is it advisable to delete these forms from your signing.

LIFE IN A SIGNED ENGLISH FAMILY

Tara's family began learning to sign when she was thirteen months old. At that time the family lived in Virginia, and the private hospital staff who were involved in Tara's diagnosis had just established a program for deaf children. The staff chose Signed English as the basis for their parent-infant program but used several dictionaries for reference when looking up particular signs.

Tara's parents, Ron and Collette, wanted to take a course in Signed English; however, none was offered in their area or sponsored by the parent-infant program. They began taking sign classes at a local college that focused on ASL. They took the signs that they learned in these classes and put them in English word order because they wished to model English to Tara.

Collette recalls that she found ASL grammar difficult and was comfortable using English as her basis for signing. She felt that she and her husband had no time to learn the grammar of a new language—they wanted to communicate with their daughter right away. Collette felt that Signed English met the communication goals of the family better and more conveniently.

If a conflict came up between the ASL and Signed English signs for a word, the family would select the sign that more specifically referred to the thing in question. Collette remembers, for example, that the family used the Signed English sign for *car* so that the ASL sign for *car* could be used for *drive*. "We wanted to expand Tara's vocabulary," Collette recalls. (Fluent ASL signers might object by pointing out that in ASL, the signs CAR and DRIVE are signed differently. Both signs have the same handshape, location, and orientation, but differ in their movement.) If the Signed English dictionary didn't have a sign, Collette would search in other sign dictionaries.

Ron was transferred to Kansas City when Tara was three years old. Collette visited the school districts in the surrounding area and chose the one with the sign policy that most closely matched the way the family signed. The school had a Signed English program, and at educational planning meetings Collette consistently asked that all the grammatical markers of Signed English be used with her daughter.

Tara's family owns every publication in the Signed English series. Collette thinks Tara taught herself to read at a very young age by using the Signed English storybooks for preschoolers. Tara studied the books while commuting to speech therapy with her mother.

Tara, Collette reports, has always been gifted in language arts. She never had a problem reading or writing English and now, as a ninth-grader, she uses speech without signs to communicate with hearing people. She still needs signing to understand what is said back to her, especially in the classroom and with her horseback riding lessons.

Collette says Tara isn't a proficient ASL user. The deaf adults to whom Tara has been exposed all have used some form of English signing, so she has never had a problem interacting with them. About ten thousand deaf people live in her community. Tara has had plenty of opportunities to converse with deaf, adult role models who use some form of English signing and ASL.

Collette feels that it was important that the family chose a method of communication and stayed with it. She credits Signed English with giving Tara the English language base she needed to succeed academically.

LEARNING SIGNED ENGLISH

When Signed English was developed, so too were many materials for parents, teachers, and others wishing to learn it. These materials, which are available from Gallaudet University Press, are especially appropriate for use with deaf children at the preschool through lower elementary levels. For example, the press offers a very comprehensive Signed English dictionary and three levels of storybooks for preschoolers.

The presentation of signs in English word order is important in implementing the Signed English approach, as is the use of the sign markers. If you cannot find a sign for a concept you wish to express, you might first check with your child's teacher to see which signs are used at the school. You can also check with members of the local Deaf community to determine what signs for local establishments, holidays, and foods prevail outside the school. Consistency in sign usage is beneficial to a deaf child just learning a new concept. Until the concept is mastered the child may be confused if presented with more than one sign for it. As with any type of signing, it is a good policy to ask your child's school to inform parents about the signs the school uses for certain subjects and stories.

NOTES

1. At the time the first edition of the Signed English dictionary was written, Harry Bornstein, Karen Saulnier, and Lillian Hamilton all worked at Gallaudet University. Gallaudet University is the only liberal arts university in the world for deaf students.

2. Bornstein 1990.
3. Ibid., 128.
4. Ibid., 129.
5. Ibid., 128.
6. Ibid., 136.
7. Bornstein 1990.

8

CONTACT SIGNING

Why Parents May Want to Learn
Contact Signing

- *Contact signing is often used when hearing and deaf people sign to one another.*
- *Contact signing is commonly used in the Deaf community.*
- *Many teachers of deaf children use contact signing.*
- *Contact signing is most often based on English word order.*

THE TERM *contact signing* is relatively new—it came into use in sign language research in the late 1980s. When this type of signing was first studied by linguists in the early 1970s it was called Pidgin Sign English (PSE).[1] Contact signing is a mixture of ASL and English, usually based on English word order. It often serves as a buffer between the two languages—a mode of communication between users of English who know some ASL and users of ASL who know some English.[2] Other common terms for contact signing are *sign English* and *conceptually accurate sign English* (CASE).

One reason for the change in terminology is that contact signing has too many ASL characteristics to be classified as an English-based pidgin.[3] Typically, a pidgin uses the vocabulary of one language and the grammar of another or is a reduced form of one language. Contact signing uses ASL vocabulary and English word order, but it incorporates many ASL grammatical features.

Another reason for the change is that the newer term more aptly suggests the circumstances in which contact signing arises and the many variations that it can take. When used by a person whose first language is English, contact signing means putting ASL signs in English word order with elements of English grammar left out and ASL features added. This is the perspective of hearing parents and deaf people who acquire proficiency in English before learning to sign. But contact signing is also used by Deaf people whose first language is ASL. For them it means omitting some of ASL's grammatical features and adding some English ones to organize the ASL signs. Contact signing takes various forms along a spectrum, depending on the users' knowledge of ASL and English. The point is that people blend features of the two languages to make communication easier.

Because contact signing is not a created sign system like manually coded English (MCE) or a sign language like ASL, educators have yet to define its role in the classroom. Contact signing can help a child learn ASL vocabulary, but is it a good vehicle for conveying the grammatical characteristics of either ASL or English? We simply do not know. Is it a stepping stone, or does its incomplete representation of both English and ASL make it a poor language model for deaf children? Certainly, more research is needed before we can assess the influence of contact signing on the language development of deaf children.[4]

THE CHARACTERISTICS OF CONTACT SIGNING

Hearing adults who are just learning to sign have a natural inclination to improvise—to try to create as much communication as they can from the few signs that they know. For example, the following sentence achieves a practical purpose: MOMMY TELL DADDY YOU GO IN TWO MINUTES. This is close to the English sentence *Mommy will tell Daddy that you are going in two minutes* and is likely to succeed in delivering that message to a deaf child. Beginning signers find it easy to communicate by stringing signs together in English word order. We can imagine a young child signing, DADDY, YOU GO IN TWO MINUTES? Daddy responds, *Yes, Daddy will go in two minutes.*

The child may not yet know the signs for *will* and *that* and other words, but what he or she does know is readily used for communication, and the father models back a complete response.

Context is important in this kind of signing. For example, if the first sentence is taken out of context, there may be some doubt as to whether the signer means *In two minutes, Mommy will tell Daddy that you are going,* or *Mommy will tell Daddy that in two minutes you are going.* But when the sentence is used in real life the child should have no trouble understanding which meaning is intended. An ASL or MCE user will get the message just as easily, although perhaps while frowning at the grammar. In ASL it would be more proper to sign the sentence as follows: MOMMY TELL DADDY, TWO-MINUTES YOU GO. Even this sentence may be incomplete if the signer neglects to include appropriate nonmanual signals to supplement the meaning of the signs.

Signing can be either literal or conceptual, and signers can switch between these two methods. Literal signing is focused on form and is a representation of each word—a verbatim translation. In a literal signing of *It's raining cats and dogs,* for example, each word and inflectional marker is signed. Conceptual signing emphasizes the meaning and is not always an exact representation of each word or phrase. In a conceptual signing of the phrase *raining cats and dogs,* a person might use signs that convey the meaning *it is raining heavily.* One way of doing this is to sign RAIN repeatedly while accompanying it with facial expressions and body movement that indicate that something is intense.

ASL and contact signing are conceptual for the most part (SEE signing tends to be literal). Contact signers can switch between literal and conceptual signing depending on their conversational partners, their desired emphasis in the moment, and their ability to sign. However, in both types of contact signing the basis is English word order, with an infusion of ASL grammatical characteristics. How much ASL is infused will depend on how much ASL the signer knows.

The Role of English

While following English word order, contact signing seldom includes English inflections such as past tense markers *(-ed)*, adverbial forms *(-ly)*, and third-person-singular verb endings *(-s)*. Words such as *a, an,* and *the* are not essential in contact signing. Even the various forms of the verb *to be* (*is, are, am,* and so on) are optional in contact signing. Some signers use a single sign, TRUE, for all forms of the verb *to be*.

You are probably wondering why it is okay to leave so much English out of contact signing when these elements are critical to spoken and printed English. After all, doesn't their absence distort the meaning of the signed sentences? Because contact signing requires a rudimentary knowledge of English, adult signers are often able to infer the complete English equivalent of a message. When you see the sentence *The boy hit the green ball,* you know that the word *green* is an adjective and that it modifies the word *ball.* You know that *green* has nothing to do with the color of the boy. We don't know whether deaf children who have not acquired a dominant language yet can fill in these gaps in the same way.

Let's take the contact signing sentence BOY CATCH GREEN BALL (see figure 22), which we will say is being used to describe what a boy just did. Assuming English is the model, this sentence is missing *the* in two places and should have the past tense of the verb. But as you know, contact signing allows more than one way to sign something, depending on whether the signer's first language is English or ASL. Consider the following examples:

English:	The alligator crawled over the land and into the pond.
Contact signing:	THE ALLIGATOR CRAWL OVER LAND AND INTO POND.
Contact signing:	ALLIGATOR CRAWL OVER LAND AND INTO POND.

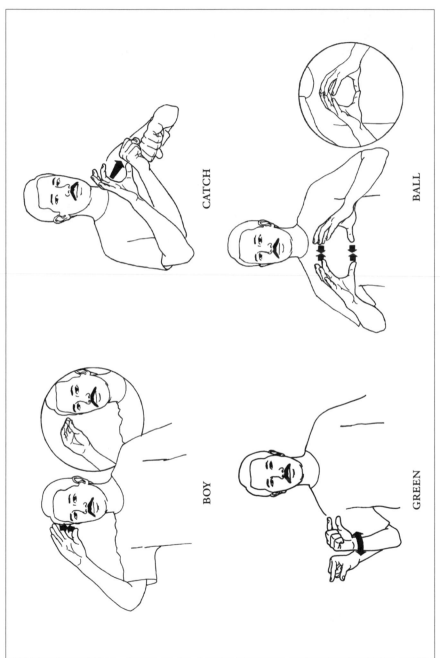

FIGURE 22. The sentence, *The boy caught the green ball*, signed in contact signing.

Contact signing: ALLIGATOR CRAWL OVER LAND INTO POND.

It is not uncommon for contact signers to voice or mouth in English a complete form of the sentence they are signing. Deaf children familiar with English can often speechread the English words missing in the signed version.

The Role of ASL

A large proportion of the signs used in contact signing are ASL signs, which generally are placed in English word order. (Some contact signers also use a few signs from Signed English and Signing Exact English.) But the word order in contact signing is sometimes influenced by the grammatical structure of ASL, as in the following example: MY SON ASK-ME FOR KEY TO BLUE CAR. The single sign ASK-ME is shown in figure 23. This type of sign, known as a *directional verb,* illustrates one of the grammatical features of ASL. Directional verbs can be signed in various directions in order to incorporate the indirect object of a sentence into the verb. In the sentence above, the signer does not explicitly sign the pronoun *me.* Instead, he or she relies on the movement of the sign ASK to convey this information. Changing the direction in which the sign ASK is made generates ASK-ME, ASK-HIM, ASK-THEM, and so forth. Other ASL characteristics that can be included in contact signing include negative incorporation, number incorporation, and the use of nonmanual signals (see chapter 4).

To illustrate another way that ASL structure may be used in contact signing, let's change the above sentence to MY SON ASK-ME FOR KEY TO CAR BLUE. The phrase *car blue* obviously is not correct English. But in ASL there is nothing unusual about placing the adjective after the noun. Doing this in the above sentence does not make it an ASL sentence, however, because the basic structure of the sentence is still English.

The mixture of English and ASL features in contact signing

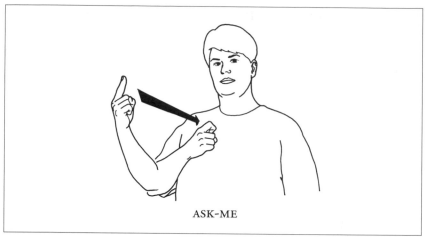

ASK-ME

FIGURE 23. By changing the direction of certain verbs, the signer can incorporate the indirect object of the verb in the sign.

varies widely depending on the user. When ASL structure plays a major role, the result is sometimes called Pidgin ASL.

WHO USES CONTACT SIGNING?

For some people contact signing is the most effective way of signing in English word order, even though it doesn't code English grammar precisely as it is spoken or written. Nearly everyone who signs uses contact signing at one time or another. It is used by a majority of teachers of deaf children in their everyday interactions with students. In fact, many Deaf people often use contact signing when conversing among themselves. It may be the way you sign if you are just a beginning signer or if your knowledge of English heavily influences your signing. Many Deaf people use contact signing with hearing signers because most hearing people they encounter do not understand ASL well enough to carry on a conversation in it. For most parents, the English word order of contact signing and the speech movements that usually accompany it make it much easier to understand than ASL. It is also easier for some Deaf people to understand contact signing than it is for them to understand a sentence signed in straight English or incorrectly in ASL.

Some research suggests that the more education Deaf people have and the more fluent they are in English, the more likely they are to use contact signing in formal situations such as the classroom or at professional gatherings.[5] We know of Deaf adults who prefer contact signing over any other type of signing. It is especially useful when a Deaf person is using an interpreter because it reduces the likelihood of errors. Most sign language interpreters are themselves native English speakers, and many are better at translating signs presented in English word order than switching from ASL to English. Interpreting ASL requires a good deal more analysis of what is being said before a message can be delivered in speech. By using contact signing Deaf people can facilitate the interpretation process.

Another important group of contact signers is adults who have become deaf after acquiring fluency in English. They usually are comfortable expressing themselves in English word order.

SPEECH AND CONTACT SIGNING

Many people who use contact signing are dependent on speech as their main means of communication. This includes hearing people, such as parents and teachers of deaf children, and deaf people who are comfortable using speech to communicate. When these people sign they often do so in conjunction with speech. This is another form of simultaneous communication, like that used with MCE but generally considered easier to use. While it is certainly possible to sign in MCE and speak at the same time, it is challenging to do it smoothly. The attempt to sign every spoken word and affix may slow down the rate of speech, which can make communication unwieldy and uncomfortable. As a result, one tends to sign only some of the words being spoken. The words omitted in signing usually are those not essential to the meaning of the sentence, as in the examples discussed earlier in this chapter. The sentence that remains is contact signing.

The simultaneous expression of signs and speech involves another adjustment in signing: the signing space tends to become smaller than that used to sign ASL. To some extent, the flow of speech dictates the speed and size of the signs, which are cut short to keep pace with the speech.

In this as in other ways, the contact signing of deaf and hearing people tends to differ. Deaf people are more likely to leave out the speech component or simply mouth key words in their contact signing sentences. In such cases the nature of the signs themselves dictates how they are formed and the speed with which they are produced. The entire meaning that the signer is trying to convey is embedded in the signs and nonmanual features that accompany them. On the other hand, when speech is involved the speaker uses pitch and intonations along with the words and may neglect the subtler aspects of signing. If the speaker focuses on both speech and signing, both are likely to be less effective than when used alone. Still, there are many people who can converse effectively in simultaneous communication.

Is Contact Signing ASL?

The widespread use of contact signing has led to the assertion that most of what we call contact signing is in fact ASL.[6] The reasoning behind this view is basically that if contact signing is part of the way Deaf people sign then it must be part of ASL. What we can say definitively is that contact signing is a middle ground where signers from different language backgrounds can communicate comfortably. Until a new definition and name for contact signing are agreed upon, parents will have to determine for themselves what educational value contact signing has for their child.

LIFE IN A CONTACT SIGNING FAMILY

Our story of a contact signing family is a rather common one in that many families use contact signing as their preferred means of signing. Convenience in signing is the reason Deana and Jed use contact signing with their deaf son, Roger. When Roger was diagnosed as deaf at the age of eighteen months, Deana registered for a signing class offered through a night school program. Like many of the signing courses taught in the 1970s and 1980s, this one covered ASL sign vocabulary but very little ASL grammar. By the end of the course Deana had learned about 350 signs.

This initial block of signs became the main body of Deana's signed vocabulary because she never took another signing course. She taught Jed how to fingerspell and sign. Later, as Roger got older he was able to teach his parents some signs. For the most part, though, the parents relied on fingerspelling and speech to fill in the gaps.

Deana and Jed are aware of ASL and the various manual codes for English. Roger's school program uses Signed English and offers an occasional Signed English workshop for parents. Deana attended one of the workshops but felt uncomfortable having to sign English words and word endings that she usually left out in contact signing. She found that signing every element of speech made it hard to concentrate on what she was saying. Jed never attended any of the workshops.

Although Deana and Jed acknowledged the possible benefits of manually coded English, they felt that Roger was doing well without it. Roger is partially integrated in a public school with interpreters and meets with a teacher of the deaf every day to work on his English language skills.

Deana and Jed say that contact signing was easy for them to learn. They are not concerned about teaching Roger ASL or English. They believe that he gets enough exposure to ASL from socializing with his deaf friends at school and enough exposure to English through Signed English in the special class at school.

CONTACT SIGNING IN SCHOOLS

So why don't all educators endorse the use of contact signing as the preferred means of communication in their classrooms? The reason is that the type of signing a teacher uses has educational value in itself. Because deaf children, especially at the lower grade levels, ordinarily do not demonstrate typical development of English meaning and form, teaching them English is a major goal in school programs. One way to teach a language is to use it in day-to-day interactions inside and outside the classroom. The signing part of contact signing does not provide a model of grammatically correct English, which children need to read and write proficiently. (A similar logic applies to schools where ASL is taught as a first language: Contact signing is not endorsed because it does not model ASL in grammatically correct form.)

The difference between English grammar and the typical grammar of contact signing is often blamed when deaf children's English skills do not improve as expected. Critics of contact signing believe that what deaf children see in signing is what they learn and that this shows up in their writing. Although there is some evidence to support this allegation, more research is needed to assess the relationship between language learning and contact signing.

Why, then, is contact signing used by so many teachers of deaf children? There are several reasons in addition to its usefulness and its compatibility with simultaneous speech. Few school districts set signing standards or guide teachers in their choice of communication mode. Many teachers lack formal training in signing or have had only a single signing course.

LEARNING CONTACT SIGNING

Most books on contact signing are research-oriented.[7] To the best of our knowledge, only a few are designed to teach the use of contact signing. *Signs of the Times,* by Edgar Shroyer, is one such book.

Most interpreter preparation programs teach their students how to distinguish between ASL, contact signing, and manually coded English. While we are unaware of any contact signing courses at colleges or other institutions, we know that in reality many instructors simply teach ASL sign vocabulary and let their students use the signs in English word order, which results in a form of contact signing.

Without a doubt the best way to learn contact signing is to interact with people who use it. This shouldn't be hard to do, as most Deaf adults switch to contact signing with hearing people. Videotapes are also helpful; some are designed specifically to teach contact signing.

NOTES

1. For more information about Pidgin Sign English or contact signing, see Woodward 1973, a seminal work, and Lucas 1989.

2. Lucas 1989; Woodward 1973

3. Lane, Hoffmeister, and Bahan 1996.

4. See Woodward 1990 for a report on the use of contact signing in the education of deaf students. Woodward coined the term Pidgin Sign English in a 1973 article; in his latest work he uses the term Sign English.

5. Lucas and Valli 1989.

6. Bragg 1990; Kuntze 1990

7. For an in-depth discussion of contact signing, see Lucas 1989; Lucas and Valli 1989; Woodward 1990.

2

THE LAW AND SIGNING

What Parents Should Know
about the Law and Signing

◆ *A school must provide signing for a deaf child if the school and the parents agree that the child will not have meaningful access to instruction without the use of a signed language.*
◆ *There are no laws that force schools to use a particular kind of signing.*
◆ *The Individualized Family Service Plan (IFSP) can be used to help parents learn signing while their deaf child is an infant and toddler.*
◆ *The Individualized Education Plan (IEP) can be used to help parents set language and signing goals for their deaf child beginning at age three.*
◆ *The law works best when parents and schools work together.*

UNDER FEDERAL LAW your child is entitled to a free, appropriate education. Signing is recognized by the law as one condition of appropriateness for many deaf children. However, school programs for deaf children are free to select the type of signing that they will offer. Many if not most programs have no written communication policy governing the use of signs. The choice often depends on teachers' personal preferences and opinions. While parents in most states cannot dictate the type of signing that a program uses with their deaf child, as vital members of the child's educational team they can exert influence in a number of ways.

THE COMPONENTS OF SCHOOL PROGRAMS
THAT USE SIGNS

We believe the following are essential elements of school programs that use signs successfully:

1. A written policy that clearly describes the type of signing that will be used by all teachers and support personnel. The program may endorse just one type of signing or more than one.
2. Clear standards for the signing skills of teachers and support personnel.
3. Procedures for evaluating the signing skills of teachers and support personnel.
4. Professional development activities that help teachers and support personnel gain fluency in a particular type of signing.
5. Sign classes offered at the school for deaf children and their families to teach them the type of signing advocated by the program.
6. Periodic review of the school's policies on signed communication.

The few schools that have signing policies tend to be schools for deaf children and public schools with large enrollments of deaf students. Of these, some have teachers and support personnel who are good signers and meet the policy standards; many do not.

For the past three decades, most programs that are committed to signing have adopted a total communication philosophy. In total communication programs the way teachers communicate is guided by the communication needs of their students. This usually means that the teachers use a combination of signs, fingerspelling, speech, audition, and print as they attempt to make themselves understood. Total communication programs do not necessarily customize their approach for the individual child, but often choose a single type of sign communication for the entire program.

Simultaneous communication is a key component of the total communication philosophy, which makes the adoption of English signing critical. Therefore, total communication policies often endorse a specific kind of signing, such as Signed English or Signing Exact English. American Sign Language may or may not be included; if it is, typically it has a supportive role and is not used as the primary language of instruction. Conversely, ASL is the only acceptable means of signing in most bilingual-bicultural programs.

Even in programs that have clear communication policies, the staff are rarely evaluated on their signing abilities or on their adherence to the policies. Parents should be on the alert for inconsistencies between what programs say they do and what actually happens in the classroom.

A school can use various strategies to ensure that its communication policy is implemented correctly:

- ◆ Hiring only teachers and interpreters who are already fluent in the appropriate type of signing,
- ◆ Promoting professional development, for example, by encouraging teachers to attend workshops on how to use signs more effectively in the classroom,
- ◆ Offering in-class support systems, such as visits by teachers to each other's classrooms in order to establish consistency in signing throughout the program, and
- ◆ Requiring staff to participate in state-level evaluations and certification opportunities.

Your school district or your child's school may have a clear policy on signing. If this is the case, then do look into it even if the type of signing prescribed is different from the kind you would like to see used with your child. At the very least, you will gain an understanding of how others view this type of signing and how a school's instructional program may benefit from the use of a single type of signing for all students.

Most parents endorse the type of signing used by the school their child happens to attend because signing is unknown territory to them. Accepting the signing advocated by the school may be a wise decision, especially if the program is good and the parents make a strong effort to become fluent signers. In any case, it is unusual for a school to change its stance on signing at the urging of just a parent or two. However, if many of the parents ask for a change, program personnel may be willing to accommodate them if they understand why the change is necessary. Whatever you as a parent decide, you should always work closely with the teachers and administrators of the school and make sure they understand your concerns about signing.

HOW THE LAW AFFECTS SIGNING
IN THE CLASSROOM

A number of state laws have changed the face of education for deaf children over the past two decades. None of these laws specifically address the kinds of signing that can be used. Rather, they establish procedures for determining the kind of educational plan that will best meet the needs of each deaf child. Because most deaf children need signing to develop an age-appropriate language base and, therefore, gain access to classroom instruction, schools are obligated to offer it and to consider which type of signing best suits their students. Unfortunately, little is known about the relationship between type of signing and educational achievement.

If the law favors no particular forms of signing, how on earth can you use it to shape a program to benefit your child? Simply stated, the law mandates that an Individualized Education Plan (IEP) be drawn up for each child requiring special education services. The IEP describes learning objectives, that is, what the child is going to learn in the coming school year; strategies that will be used to help the child accomplish these objectives; and evaluation procedures for determining whether or not the objectives have been achieved. This plan must be signed by a parent. A parent who disagrees with the IEP signs it in a place that indicates dissent. Parents can also indicate that they want the program to resolve the areas of disagreement. It is with the IEP that parents exert their most powerful influence on school programming (examples are provided later in this chapter).

The state laws that established this degree of parental influence followed the passage of federal laws that gave deaf children a legal right to be identified, evaluated, and educated in the most appropriate manner. (As strange as it may seem, the federal laws were needed because many children with hearing loss are identified only after they begin school and have already suffered a significant delay in their education and language development.)

The main impact of the federal laws was to allow deaf children to be educated in a variety of settings. Up until the late 1970s, the majority of deaf children were sent routinely to state residential schools. A small percentage attended neighborhood schools without appropriate support and services. Today about 80 percent of all deaf children are enrolled in public school programs in their own home communities.[1] The number and typical size of schools for deaf children has declined drastically over the past two decades. Consequently, today's signing policies seldom apply to a large body of deaf students; rather they exist in some programs and not in others. While this dispersion may be detrimental to the quality of deaf education in the long run, it works in favor of parents who want to see a particular type of signing used in their child's program. We encourage parents to use existing laws to try to ensure that their deaf children are exposed to the kinds of signing that are best for them. These laws have given parents a chance to take an active role in the education of their children.

The Individuals with Disabilities Education Act

The Individuals with Disabilities Education Act (IDEA),[2] or Public Law 105-17, is a 1997 amendment of a law passed in 1975 requiring that children with disabilities be educated in the least restrictive environment, which is often interpreted as the home school district. The earlier law was called the Education for All Handicapped Children Act (Public Law 94-142). It was amended by Public Law 101-476 in 1990. Before the passage of PL 94-142, only about 50 percent of children with disabilities were receiving the special education services that they needed in public schools; the rest were being taught in segregated educational facilities.

The most important guarantees of IDEA are listed below.[3] Each has implications for children who sign.

1. *Full service at no cost.* All children who have been identified as deaf must be provided with a free and appropriate public education, regardless of the extent of their disability. The type of education, signing or oral, for example, does not affect implementation of this requirement of the law. Therefore, school districts are obligated to meet the communication demands of the deaf students whom they serve—they cannot turn a deaf child away simply because they don't have a signing program or will need to construct one.

2. *Nondiscriminatory evaluation.* Each student must be fairly and accurately evaluated. This means that tests must be appropriate to the child's cultural and linguistic background. If a student's primary means of communication is signing, then tests are to be administered to the student in the type of signed communication to which the student is accustomed. Nondiscriminatory evaluation also means that the selected tests are chosen at a level that will accurately measure the child's aptitude and achievement levels.

3. *Individualized Education Plan (IEP).* An IEP must be written, implemented, and evaluated for each deaf student. The components of the IEP are specified in the law, but IEP forms differ from program to program, which may be confusing to parents who move to a new school district.

Each IEP is to be developed in a conference attended by the parents; a teacher of the deaf or a special education teacher; a regular education teacher if the child takes classes in general education classrooms; a school district representative, who is usually the coordinator of services for deaf children throughout the district; and other personnel (such as speech therapists and audiologists) deemed necessary to the determination of a suitable educational plan for the child.

If the parents agree with the plan drawn up, they sign the IEP and the program is implemented and reviewed at the end of the school year. If the parents do not agree, they can indicate their disagreement and their decision either to allow the program to be implemented or to pursue due process and hope that a change is ordered by an impartial hearing officer assigned by the state.

4. *Least restrictive environment (LRE).* The law states that deaf children should be given a free, appropriate education in the least restrictive environment. Professionals working with children with special needs other than deafness often see public school programs as the least restrictive environment. For deaf children, however, a public school program may in fact be a restrictive environment because of the isolation from meaningful social and communication interactions. The LRE for a deaf child can be determined only when the child's particular needs are identified. Then goals and objectives can be written to meet the targeted needs, and the supports and services necessary to facilitate learning can be discussed. Finally, a placement is chosen in which these supports and services are available. This may be a school for deaf children, a classroom in a neighboring public school district, or a local school.

5. *Mediation and due process.* Parents have the legal right to be consulted about their child's educational program prior to its implementation, the right to obtain an individual evaluation from a qualified examiner outside the school system, and the right to request mediation or due process hearings when they disagree with all or part of the educational plan for their child. Mediation and due process hearings are meant to ensure fairness and accountability. It is

during these hearings that parents provide verification for whatever complaints they wish to submit, for example, that the goals and objectives written for their child have not been met, that the supports and services to be provided have not been put in place, or that their input as parents has not been used.

Mediation and due process are costly and time-consuming processes. The wait for a final decision can last as long as a year. If the parents win, all of the costs associated with the case are covered by the school district. If the parents lose, they must cover their own expenses, including legal fees. These expenses may include the hiring of a lawyer or a person who is willing to advocate on behalf of the parents, travel, photocopying of written materials, and the hiring of expert witnesses. It is common for parents to request an evaluation by an outside examiner, which may involve bringing someone in from out of state; in that case, airfare, meals, and accommodations must be covered as well as the evaluator's fee.

Given the expense and time involved in due process, it is highly desirable that parents establish a rapport with school personnel. They should try to resolve any concerns before the drafting of the IEP. But parents should not back away from a due process hearing if they feel that their child is not receiving a proper education and if they can provide evidence to support their position.

6. *Parental participation.* Under the law parents are guaranteed access to their child's school records. It is also their responsibility to attend educational meetings regarding their child. If these are held at an inconvenient time, parents can request a different time. Parents should be prepared to offer suggestions for IEP objectives. In order to become informed participants, parents can learn about deaf education by meeting with other parents; reading professional journals such as the *American Annals of the Deaf, Perspectives in Deaf Education,* and the *Journal of Deaf Studies and Deaf Education,* and magazines such as *Exceptional Parent;* joining parent organizations such as the American Society for Deaf Children; and searching for Web sites in the field.

The Elements of an Individualized Education Plan

The IEP is a planning document and you, as a parent, are an important part of the team that puts it together. Each state has its own IEP form and each must include at least the following components:

1. *A statement of the child's current level of performance.* The IEP must include an accurate description of the effects of deafness on the child's present academic performance (e.g., in language, reading, math, science) and nonacademic performance (e.g., self-reliance, intelligence, social skills, vocational abilities). Scores on standardized tests are also included; these can help parents and school personnel judge the child's progress from one year to the next. The IEP should contain both formal and informal data to document the child's skills. When the IEP is written, the information must be no more than two months old and should be provided to parents in a written report.

2. *A statement of annual goals.* Annual goals describe what will be accomplished in the coming year. They are based on the current level of performance and usually are stated in broad terms. They reflect realistic expectations of performance changes in each area of academic or social need, including an assessment of the amount of time and type of instruction necessary for achieving the goal. Some appropriate annual goals might be:

- Danny will complete second-grade math.
- Carlos will move from third- to fourth-grade reading material.
- Min-Hua will be able to communicate with her peers during daily classroom activities.

These goals are stated in general, even ambiguous, terms. Their purpose is to indicate the general direction of progress.

3. *A statement of short-term instructional objectives.* Short-term objectives are stated in measurable terms so that it can be determined whether they have been accomplished, and they are arranged in sequence to show how the annual goals will be attained. The short-term

objectives are used to guide instructional activities. The following are examples of measurable objectives:

- Mohammed will add one-digit numbers to two-digit numbers with carrying, with 90 percent accuracy.
- José will use signs to initiate conversations with his peers on a daily basis.
- Kim will read a basal story at the second-grade level every week and answer three comprehension questions correctly.

Each of these objectives gives the teacher a basis for the planning of student activities.

4. *A statement of the specific educational services or materials needed by the child.* The designation of instructional supports and services to be provided to the child is a critical aspect of the IEP, especially with regard to signing. The IEP may require that the child receive interpreting services for all school activities, including lunch, recess, assemblies, and extracurricular activities. It may require that the interpreter be kept informed of the student's English and/or ASL language needs. The classroom seating arrangements may be specified to give deaf children a better view so that they can communicate with the rest of the class. The IEP may require that signing classes be offered for hearing children and teachers and that books about signing be purchased for the library.

The IEP also indicates related services—special programs, which may be developmental, corrective, or supportive in nature, that are not part of the special or general education program. These might include speech therapy, physical or occupational therapy, transportation, and counseling services. A student who has poorly developed signing skills may need a tutor or a specially designed signing program.

The choice of a school is based on a child's needs for supports and services. The child's needs should be matched with the program that can best provide the appropriate services, including the most appropriate kind of signing.

5. *A statement of how the child will participate in a general education program.* The IEP indicates academic and social areas where the student can benefit from interacting with hearing peers and specifies the amount of time to be spent in that way. Examples range from mainstreaming in formal academic subjects to spending time with hearing students in the lunchroom, in school assemblies, and on the playground.

6. *Procedures for measuring progress toward the objectives.* The IEP includes evaluation procedures, criteria, and schedules. Evaluations may be scheduled for each week, month, semester, or year, but an objective assessment of the child's progress must be made. A notebook sent home to parents weekly is the typical method of informing parents about their child's progress at school. This process facilitates the determination of new goals and the accompanying objectives, the revision of current activities, and the selection of effective teaching strategies. The IEP should specify the assessment instruments, that is, the testing methods or procedures that will be used to gather data on the child's progress. The instruments must be appropriate for the child and must have a reliable track record.

Vague or subjective measurement procedures should not be used. Parents should not simply accept teachers' hunches or personal opinions about their child's progress and needs, but should demand that teachers back up their assertions with the results of both formal and informal testing. Data collected on a regular basis and used to make decisions should be compiled and explained to the parents before each IEP meeting. The type of data collected will depend on the reasons for testing. Examples of data that may be included in the annual review are achievement test scores, assessments of signing skills, checklists for other skills, attendance data, records of direct observation, curriculum-based assessments, and permanent examples of the student's work.

7. *The date services will begin and the amount of time involved.* The IEP includes a schedule of services. For example, it might state

that sign instruction will begin on 9/15/98 and will occur three times per week throughout the school year, and that each session will last for twenty minutes.

The IEP must be reviewed once a year, at which time the appropriateness of educational placement and services can be reconsidered. If the student's progress indicates the need for a change in placement or services, by law the change must be made. As an example, let's say that last year your child began to learn to sign and was in a self-contained preschool program with a teacher of the deaf serving as the primary teacher. This year your child was placed in a general education kindergarten and is the only deaf child. An interpreter has been provided, but your child is having trouble understanding her. Your child's first semester progress was poor. An IEP meeting is called and it is decided that your child requires the services of a trained teacher of the deaf who will be able to sign in a consistent manner and at a pace that the child can follow. Once the IEP has the necessary signatures, including that of one parent, the change can occur. An IEP does not guarantee academic success. It does, however, ensure that a child will progress, that the services and materials the child needs will be provided, and that the child will be placed in an appropriate setting. Parents have the right to call their child's educational team together whenever they have concerns.

The Education of the Handicapped Act Amendments Law

Another important law for deaf children is Public Law 99-457, an amendment to the federal Education of the Handicapped Act. Congress passed PL 99-457 in September 1986, after gathering evidence that preschoolers with disabilities who received early intervention did better in school later on. In essence, this law gave to preschoolers (ages three to five) what IDEA provided for schoolchildren (ages five to twenty-one). In place of the IEP, PL 99-457 calls for an Individualized Family Service Plan (IFSP).

This law can make a big difference for parents of young deaf children. The preschool years are critical for the development of language skills, and PL 99-457 provides parents with the help they may require to ensure optimal development. The law does not require that parents send their deaf preschoolers to school; it helps parents who decide to do so by bringing them into the education process.

Parents no longer have to wait until the kindergarten years to determine which type of signed communication is best for their deaf child. Under PL 99-457 they can get support early to begin signing and to spur on the development of their child's language and thinking skills.

The Elements of the Individualized Family Service Plan

The Individualized Family Service Plan (IFSP), a contract drawn up between the family and the school district under Public Law 99-457, is similar to an IEP. The IFSP calls for a multidisciplinary assessment, that is, an evaluation conducted by professionals from diverse disciplines, such as a teacher of the deaf, a speech-language pathologist, an audiologist, a director of special education services, and other appropriate personnel. Although families are not required to send their children to preschool or to obtain early intervention services for their deaf children, if they choose to do so an IFSP must be created.

The services provided may include special education; speech, signing, and language services for the toddler; audiological services; parent and family training and counseling services; medical and health services; and so forth. Communication experts can help parents use the home environment to develop their deaf child's signing and language skills. All of these services are provided at no cost to the family. Like IEP forms, IFSP forms differ from one state to the next.

MAKING IEPS AND IFSPS WORK FOR YOU

Always try to make sure that the goals and objectives in your child's IEPs and IFSPs are reasonable. This is the only way to ensure that they will be implemented. Also be sure that the type of signing you desire is specified and is reflected in the objectives as well as the goals. Some appropriate objectives might be that your preschool child will learn to articulate signs clearly, and use three- or four-word phrases or sentences in grammatically correct English (or ASL). At the elementary level your objectives might be that your child learn to use correctly formed past-tense verbs in writing, and name ten professions by using the correct signs for labeling them. Objectives should be worded specifically enough to indicate important aspects of the way your child needs to be taught. For instance, when stories are read to the class, should they be paraphrased in signs, signed precisely in English, or translated into ASL?

Your communication objective can stipulate that signs always be used, speech always be audible, a certified interpreter always be present, or whatever else may be needed to promote effective communication at school. You can also request that the comments and questions of your child's classmates in public school always be signed if an interpreter is present. This ensures that your deaf child is included in social conversations and takes part in the cultural life of his or her peers. Similarly, in a school for deaf children, objectives can be written that facilitate the exposure of your child to the form of communication that you feel best suits his or her educational needs. For example, it might be stipulated that a qualified interpreter accompany the class on field trips, or that your child's primary means of communication, if different from that of the general student body, be accommodated in the classroom and at all assemblies.

The IEP has a section for programmatic considerations. This is the place to indicate that adults with signing skills who work at your child's school should always sign in the presence of your child, that sign classes should be taught to hearing students in the school, that an interpreter should be provided for lunch and recess periods, that the child's interpreter arrive fifteen minutes before school and stay fifteen minutes after school in order to talk with team members, prepare for future assignments, and address communication problems as they arise. You may want to prioritize your concerns in the IFSP or IEP and establish timetables for their implementation. Timetables are important. Not everything can happen immediately after the IFSP or IEP is signed, but if an objective is deemed worthy of listing in the plan, the school district must ensure that the personnel necessary to achieve it are in place without unnecessary delay. If deaf children are to be a real part of a school program, team members must be willing to design IFSPs and IEPs so that access to communication is optimized.

Another important point for parents to remember in discussions with school personnel is that the needs of one child should never be sacrificed to the needs of another. For example, suppose a mother asks that an interpreter be provided at lunch so that her daughter can participate in the social chatter around her. This might occur in a public school or in a school for deaf children if the child is new at the school and hasn't learned to sign fluently. The principal or teacher may respond that if an interpreter is provided at that time, another child will be deprived of needed interpreter services. This response should not intimidate the mother. She is right to take action to keep her child from being isolated during lunch. Parents must advocate for the needs of their child; schools must determine how to fulfill the IFSP and IEP objectives.

WORKING WITH YOUR SCHOOL DISTRICT

Many parents are reluctant to get involved when school districts make decisions about deaf children's education. This is the position many of them take with their hearing children, and they see no reason to act differently now that they have a deaf child in school. But there is a difference. With a deaf child there is a much greater danger that the public school environment will be inappropriate. Parents do need to be involved to make sure that the environment will help their child acquire a language and learn academically and socially.

Your school is not solely accountable if your child does not demonstrate an acceptable standard of learning. As a parent, you must take the responsibility of following your child's progress in school to help the school do its job.

Notes

1. 1997 *American Annals of the Deaf* Directory issue.

2. The National Information Center for Children and Youth with Disabilities distributes several publications about IDEA and related federal laws, for example, *Questions and Answers about the Individuals with Disabilities Act (IDEA)* (vol. 3, no. 2, 1993), and *The Education of Children and Youth with Special Needs: What Do the Laws Say?* (vol. 1, no. 1, 1991). Single copies are free. To order these and other materials, write to the National Information Center for Children and Youth with Disabilities, P.O. Box 1492, Washington, DC 20013-1492, or call 1-800-695-0285.

3. Hallahan and Kauffman 1997.

10

FORMING PARTNERSHIPS
WITH SCHOOLS

> ### What Parents Can Do
> ### to Help Their Child Learn
>
> - *Parents should get involved in their deaf child's education, at home and at school.*
> - *Parents can establish goals for their deaf child's education and make them known to the child's teachers.*
> - *Parents should work with school personnel rather than against them.*
> - *Parents can seek mediation or due process when reasonable requests they have made are not accepted by the schools.*

IF YOU, THE PARENT, are going to make decisions involving your deaf child's education, you need to be well informed. To become well informed takes legwork. If signing is important to you, then you should read about it and talk to other people with a variety of viewpoints.

You may find much contradiction in what you read and hear, but don't let that discourage you. Whether other people agree with you or not is beside the point. Your child is your child. It is for you to decide what is best for the child and the rest of the family. Nothing says you can't change your mind later. In fact, it is crucial that you keep an open mind as you watch your child develop. You will need to pay attention and continue making decisions throughout the child's schooling.

One of the most important things you can do to become an effective advocate for your child is to establish a good rapport with the personnel at your child's school. The better your relationship with the school staff, the easier it will be to discuss your goals for your child's education.

GET TO KNOW THE SCHOOL PERSONNEL

To establish a good rapport with your school, you need to know about your rights as a parent of a deaf child. Find out how much say you have in your child's education and how you can present your requirements so that people at the school take note. In this book we have offered some information about your rights, but your school principal or your child's special education teacher can give you more. They can give you the inside scoop on how an Individualized Family Service Plan (IFSP) and an Individualized Educational Plan (IEP) are planned in the school district and how to schedule one for your child (see chapter 9).

Remember, you can call your IFSP or IEP team together any time—formally or informally—to make sure that you are up to date on all matters relating to your child's education. Bring a friend to the meetings if it helps you to relax and gain a clearer perspective. Bring notes and a list of any questions you may have. Ask for clarification. Ask specific questions and keep asking until you are satisfied that you understand how your child is being educated.

Meeting the school personnel who will work with your child serves several valuable purposes. First, you let them know that you are a concerned parent and that you expect to be involved; this is a quality that most teachers desire in the parents of their students. Second, by observing in the classroom, you get to see what their day is typically like. Observing may help you to verify your fears, or it may reassure you that everything is going pretty well and there is nothing to worry about. In either case it helps you become a more effective advocate for an education that meets your child's needs. Third, by meeting school personnel you learn about their views on the education of deaf children and on the role of signing. Listen to determine if their goals match yours.

Parent meetings allow administrators, teachers, and other support personnel the opportunity to talk about what they do and their qualifications. These sessions are not the time for individual matters or emotional outbursts. Don't go to a meeting for a shoulder to cry on or to look for a scapegoat if your child is not doing as well as you hoped. This might be done over coffee with one or two other parents.

MEET WITH OTHER PARENTS

As you meet with school personnel and hear their perspectives on whatever it is you are concerned about, you can broaden your view by meeting with other parents of deaf children. Other parents can be invaluable sources of insight into the issues that you face in the day-to-day education of your deaf child. They have stories to tell that will enrich your understanding of educational alternatives. Various school districts handle things differently, and knowing how things are done elsewhere can help you in brainstorming with your child's team.

Sometimes other parents can act as sounding boards, allowing you to play out your ideas before settling upon a decision. We strongly recommend that you participate in school functions for parents. Also, look for support groups for parents of deaf children at the national and local levels. The American Society for Deaf Children (ASDC) has local chapters across the country. They publish *The Endeavor,* a newsletter for parents, and hold biannual conferences. This organization is run exclusively by parents for parents. If there is no ASDC chapter or other support group in your school district, think about forming one or driving to the nearest one in your region. Even if you don't go often, making these connections can be an important source of emotional as well as informative support. Check the

Internet too. Many parents are finding mutual support through this medium.

MEET WITH DEAF ADULTS

No matter what type of signing you are contemplating, you can find Deaf adults who will support your choice and others who will disagree. Whatever their opinions, most have experience that will be of interest to you—experience with ASL or English signing, with public schools or schools for deaf children, with good teachers or poor teachers. Listen to the stories they tell and let them become part of that grand body of knowledge that you are accumulating.

Remember, all stories are just stories. Telling a story means recalling one's own version of events, interpreting facts, injecting personal opinions, and so forth. Although a story may touch you, that doesn't mean that its message is right for these times or for your family. Nevertheless, most Deaf adults, like people in general, have good intentions and want to be a positive influence. Try to get to know them on that level. Meet with them over coffee, discuss your worries, ask them to recommend solutions, ask them to observe classes and activities at your deaf child's school.

Don't buy into advice that violates the values you uphold. When a hearing person expresses an opinion about the education of hearing children, you evaluate it in your own terms. Take the same stance when the topic is the education of deaf children, whether the person you are talking to is deaf or hearing.

PARENTS AND SCHOOLS CAN WORK TOGETHER

We have seen many stellar school programs for deaf children. Here we would like to describe just two. One has an exemplary parent program; the other has made signing part of the entire school program.

The first program has eleven deaf students from the preschool through junior high school levels. The parents of these eleven students meet every Monday evening at the elementary school to help each other with their communication skills and discuss their concerns and their children's school experiences. Also present at the meetings are the school principal, teachers from the deaf education program, and other involved personnel. Guest speakers discuss language development, how to improve thinking skills, and various aspects of deafness. Older deaf children in the program are invited to talk about the role of communication in their education. The parents and teachers have designed training programs to improve their communication skills. These parents have made the time to do what they believe is best for their deaf children. Each week they acquire more information to help them along this road.

The second program has twenty deaf students from the preschool through high school levels. The school district offers free signing classes on Monday nights for anyone who wants to attend. The special education director for the district, the deaf education supervisor (a former teacher of deaf children), and the school principal meet monthly with parents and Deaf adults in the community on an advisory board to discuss Deaf culture, signing, and Deaf awareness. They also meet with a strategic planning committee to discuss program improvement and parent concerns. The school encourages its deaf students to participate in activities at a nearby residential school for deaf children. The public school environment includes certified educational interpreters, a lead interpreter who coordinates signing to hearing peers, and a database of signs. Signing is taught daily to everyone at the school, and signs for objects are posted throughout the school. A Deaf janitor is employed there too. Steps have been taken to broaden the exposure of the hearing students and staff to Deaf culture so that they can appreciate the value of signing in the lives of Deaf people. Several times a year Deaf visitors meet with all 350 hearing and deaf students. The winner of a Deaf statewide beauty pageant, a Deaf school counselor, a Deaf mime, and other

Deaf citizens employed in a variety of fields have come to share their life stories at small group sessions or large assemblies for the entire school.

We won't pretend that these two public school programs are able to maintain the same high level of support for parents and signing every year. After all, children grow up, families move, teachers and administrators transfer to other schools. But the point is that with a healthy dose of enthusiasm and effort, a school can do more than simply teach deaf children in a classroom and send end-of-semester reports to parents.

SET GOALS FOR YOUR DEAF CHILD'S EDUCATION

What are your goals for your deaf child? Your goals will be shaped by your child's age, current level of language development (in one or more languages), amount of hearing, motivation to learn, and many other factors, including the value that you place on academic success. Make a list of the things you want your child to accomplish in school.[1] When you list the communication skills that you want your child to acquire, don't feel that you must select just one type of communication. There is nothing wrong with wanting your deaf child to sign and speak well, or wanting the child to be a fluent signer in both English and ASL. Children can be members of both the hearing and Deaf communities. Speech and signs, English and ASL are not incompatible. A deaf child who learns more than one way of communicating will have more opportunities later.

Once you have established some goals for your deaf child's education, share them with the child's teachers and other school personnel, such as speech and language specialists, and with other parents. Ideally you will be able to do this before a formal meeting with your child's education team. Your child's teachers will be better prepared to write an educational plan that meets your approval if they know your goals.

Evaluate the Program's Sign Language Policy

Parents usually have no trouble finding a school where signing will be used with their child. More than three-fourths of all students who are deaf and of school age now use some form of signing at school. What is difficult is to find programs where the type of signing parents have chosen is used consistently.

Because many schools have no mandated sign policy, it is common for teachers in the same school to sign words and phrases differently, or for interpreters to sign differently from teachers. Parents may want to work with their school team to decide which method of signing will be used with their child and to arrange for consistency in the way adults at the school will sign with the child.

In the process of choosing a type of signing and an appropriate school program, you may find it helpful to create a questionnaire for administrators, general education teachers, teachers of the deaf, interpreters, paraprofessionals, and other service providers working with deaf children in your area. Here are some examples of questions you might include:

1. What is the policy of your school district with regard to sign use? That is, are school personnel supposed to be using ASL, Signed English, SEE, contact signing, or some other type of signing?
2. Do personnel at your school all use the same language or sign system? If not, what are the advantages and disadvantages of this approach for deaf students?
3. Are school personnel consistent in the way they use a particular method of signing, whatever it may be?
4. Can school personnel evaluate their English signing? Would they complete the following exercise?

   > Please circle the words or parts of words in the following sentences that you probably would not sign or not sign exactly as they appear here. For example, if you would not sign the word *the* in the first

sentence, circle that word. If you would sign *think* instead of *thought,* circle that word.

   a. Peter thought that his mother's smile was as bright as the Saturday sunshine.

   b. All day long, Peter helped his dad out with the chores.

   c. With his books neatly put away in the den and the familiar smoke detector hung in the hall upstairs, the new house really was beginning to feel like home.

   d. Peter had kept hoping that it wouldn't be long before he'd be the proud owner of a puppy.

   e. The mutt was skinny and a strange rust color.

   f. Peter ordered her to heel as he reached for the door.[2]

5. The sentences above are typical of stories an adult might read to a child. How do you think a deaf child will learn to use the words and phrases that school personnel circled above?

Many more questions might be included. Be prepared to give serious thought to the answers. The people who fill out your questionnaire all have devoted much time to arrive where they are now. Their teaching styles are shaped by the successes and failures that they have experienced. They may have very good reasons for the way they sign. Your task is to evaluate their reasons in light of the goals that you have set for your child.

Form a Signing Committee

In school districts that have no signing policy it may be advantageous to form a committee to discuss and monitor the types of signing to be used. You can suggest this at the school and offer to serve on the committee. The committee might consist of teachers, interpreters, paraprofessionals, representatives of parents' groups, and others. The committee should be of manageable size and should meet regularly—perhaps once a month in the beginning. The committee's tasks might include choosing a basic sign book for school staff and parents to use as a reference guide; deciding what signs to use for words that do not appear in the basic book, recording them in a data bank, and distributing printouts at regular intervals to parents and school personnel; assisting with the evaluations of parents', teachers', and interpreters' sign skills; and videotaping stories that are studied at school so children can review them at home.

As schools establish signing policies, they will need to develop procedures to evaluate how closely teachers and other staff follow the policies. One method is to videotape a person signing in a variety of situations. A small group of committee members and school staff might watch the tapes together and provide both positive comments and suggestions for improvement with regard to form, content, facial expression, pace of signing, clarity of signs, and so on. The person filmed might also watch the tapes to evaluate his or her own performance.

We recommend that the signing committee set no more than five goals per semester and that at least once a year the members evaluate themselves as to whether they have met those goals.

HELP YOUR DEAF CHILD SUCCEED

If you hand over to school personnel all responsibility for the education and socialization of your deaf child, you are taking a chance with your child's education and future happiness. It is unfair to your school team if you complain but don't visit the school or establish working relationships with staff. It is equally unfair if you never let teachers know how you feel about your child's progress. Teachers need feedback and your input is valuable. Let teachers know how your child is doing with homework assignments and what activities the child is involved in after school that will provide experiential background for reading and other school subjects. Also, let teachers know when you are pleased with their work. They are human too and should not be deprived of well-earned praise.

Some parents tell us that they hate to make demands of their child's teachers because they want everyone to be friends. Some fear that teachers will "take it out on the child." We have never found any justification for this fear, but we do know that friendliness doesn't do the trick. You may be friendly with your car dealer, but when things go wrong with the car, you need to bring it in and explain the problem. When things go wrong at school you should take the same approach, with confidence that you are simply being a good consumer.

Many parents are pleased with their deaf child's school and satisfied with the type of signing used in the school even if it is not what they use at home. These parents, too, should maintain contact with the school and continue to communicate their expectations in a positive manner. They may want to advocate for more frequent progress reports, for teaching of signs to hearing students and others at the school, and for the acquisition of captioned videotapes and books on signing for the school library. All of these are legitimate needs that exist in many schools.

Schools and parents must strive to work together. Ask your child's teachers what you can do at home to supplement the work being done at school. If you have the time, offer to help out in the classroom now and then. Whatever you do, stay involved in your deaf child's education. Think of your involvement as part of the total educational package.

Your deaf child's education is your education too!

NOTES

1. See Luetke-Stahlman, 1996, 1998a, and 1998b for information that may help you formulate your goals for your child.

2. These sentences are from S. Stephen, "The Dumbest Dog in the World," *Playmate Magazine*, October 1985. To order, write to Children's Playmate, Children's Better Health Institute, P.O. Box 10242, Des Moines, IA 50381.

REFERENCES

Bornstein, H. 1990. Signed English. In *Manual communication: Implications for education,* edited by H. Bornstein, 21–44. Washington, D.C.: Gallaudet University Press.

Bornstein, H., K. Saulnier, and L. Hamilton. 1975. *The Signed English dictionary: For preschool and elementary levels.* Washington, D.C.: Gallaudet University Press.

———. 1983. *The comprehensive Signed English dictionary.* Washington, D.C.: Gallaudet University Press.

Bragg, B. 1990. Communication and the Deaf community: Where do we go from here? In *Communication issues among Deaf people: A Deaf American monograph,* edited by M. Garretson, 9–14. Silver Spring, Md.: National Association of the Deaf.

Fischer, S., and P. Siple, eds. 1990. *Theoretical issues in sign language research.* Chicago: University of Chicago Press.

Groce, N. 1985. *Everyone here spoke sign language.* Cambridge: Harvard University Press.

Gustason, G. 1990. Signing Exact English. In *Manual communication: Implications for education,* edited by H. Bornstein, 108–27. Washington, D.C.: Gallaudet University Press.

Gustason, G., D. Pfetzing, and E. Zawolkow. 1973. *Signing Exact English.* Rossmoor, Calif.: Modern Signs Press.

Gustason, G., and E. Zawolkow. 1993. *Signing Exact English.* Rossmoor, Calif.: Modern Signs Press.

Hallahan, D., and J. Kauffman. 1997. *Exceptional children: Introduction to special education.* 7th ed. Boston: Allyn and Bacon.

Kuntze, M. 1990. ASL: Unity and power. In *Communication issues among Deaf people: A Deaf American monograph,* edited by M. Garretson, 75–78. Silver Spring, Md.: National Association of the Deaf.

Lane, H. 1984. *When the mind hears.* New York: Random House.

Lane, H., R. Hoffmeister, and B. Bahan. 1996. *A journey into the DEAF-WORLD.* San Diego: DawnSignPress.

Lucas, C., ed. 1989. *The sociolinguistics of the Deaf community.* New York: Academic Press.

————, ed. 1990. *Sign language research: Theoretical issues.* Washington, D.C.: Gallaudet University Press.

Lucas, C., and C. Valli. 1989. Language contact in the American Deaf community. In *The sociolinguistics of the Deaf community,* edited by C. Lucas, 11–40. New York: Academic Press.

Luetke-Stahlman, B. 1988a. Documenting syntactically and semantically incomplete bimodal input to hearing-impaired subjects. *American Annals of the Deaf* 133:230–34.

————. 1988b. Educational ramifications of various instructional inputs for hearing-impaired students. *Association of Canadian Educators of the Hearing Impaired Journal* 14:105–21.

————. 1996. *One mother's story: An educator becomes a parent.* Los Alamitos, Calif.: Modern Signs Press.

————. 1998a. *Language across the curriculum when students are deaf or hard of hearing.* Hillsboro, Ore.: Butte Publications.

————. 1998b. *Language issues in deaf education.* Hillsboro, Ore.: Butte Publications.

Luetke-Stahlman, B., and W. Milburn. 1996. Seeing Essential English. *American Annals of the Deaf* 141:29–33.

Mahshie, S. N. 1995. *Educating deaf children bilingually.* Washington, D.C.: Gallaudet University, Pre-College Programs.

Moores, D. F., T. Kluwin, R. Johnson, C. Ewoldt, P. Cox, L. Blennerhassett, L. Kelly, C. Sweet, and L. Fields. 1987. *Factors predictive of literacy in deaf adolescents with deaf parents: Factors predictive of literacy in deaf adolescents in total communication programs.* Project No. NIH-NINCDS-83-19, Contract No. N01-NS-4-2365. Final Report to the National Institute of Neurological and Communicative Disorders and Stroke.

Parish, P. 1977. *Teach us, Amelia Bedelia.* New York: Greenwillow Books.

Paul, P. 1996. Reading vocabulary knowledge and deafness. *Journal of Deaf Studies and Deaf Education* 1:3–15.

Paul, P., and S. Quigley. 1994. *Language and deafness.* 2d ed. San Diego: Singular Publishing Group.

Pinker, S. 1994. *The language instinct: How the mind creates language.* New York: William Morrow.

Quigley, S., and P. Paul. 1990. *Language and deafness.* San Diego: College-Hill Press.

Sandler, W. 1990. Temporal aspects and ASL phonology. In *Theoretical issues in sign language research,* edited by S. Fischer and P. Siple. Vol. 1, 7–35. Chicago: University of Chicago Press.

Schein, J. D., and D. A. Stewart. 1995. *Language in motion: Exploring the nature of sign.* Washington, D.C.: Gallaudet University Press.

Schick, B., and M. Moeller. 1992. What is learnable in manually coded English sign systems? *Applied Psycholinguistics* 13:313–40.

Stedt, J. D., and D. F. Moores. 1990. Manual codes on English and American Sign Language: Historical perspectives and current realities. In *Manual communication: Implications for education,* edited by H. Bornstein, 1–20. Washington, D.C.: Gallaudet University Press.

Stewart, D. A. 1987. The effects of mode and language in total communication. *Association of Canadian Educators of the Hearing Impaired Journal* 13:24–39.

Stokoe, W. C. 1978. *Sign language structure.* Rev. ed. Silver Spring, Md.: Linstok Press.

Volterra, V., and C. Erting, eds. 1994. *From gesture to language in hearing and deaf children.* Washington, D.C.: Gallaudet University Press.

Walworth, M., D. F. Moores, and T. J. O'Rourke. 1992. *A free hand.* Silver Spring, Md.: TJ Publishers.

Wilbur, R. B. 1979. *American Sign Language and sign systems.* Baltimore: University Park Press.

Woodward, J. 1973. Some characteristics of Pidgin Sign English. *Sign Language Studies,* 3:39–46.

———. 1990. Sign English in the education of deaf students. In *Manual communication: Implications for education,* edited by H. Bornstein, 67–80. Washington, D.C.: Gallaudet University Press.

INDEX

as model for English, 98–99; sign markers, 88–93, 94; tenets of, 86–87

signing space, 3, 55–57, 62, 73

sign markers, 82; in Signed English, 107–11; in Signing Exact English, 88–93, 94

signs: in ASL, 54–55, 64–65; dictionaries of, 13; elements of, 3–5; inventing of, 102; in manually coded English, 78, 79–82; nonmanual signals used with, 5–6; regional differences in, 12–13; in Signed English, 104–7; in Signing Exact English, 87–98, 101–2; *See also* sign markers

Signs of the Times (Shroyer), 128

simultaneous communication (SimCom), 25, 33–34, 82–83, 132; and contact signing, 125–26

space, signing. *See* signing space

speech: and contact signing, 125–26; cued, 26; as distinguished from language, 40; impact of signing on, 20–21; and oral movement, 30–31

Stewart, David, 74n.3

Stokoe, William, 32–33, 85

syntax, 44–45

total communication, 24–25, 33–34, 36–37, 70; in schools, 131–32

"two-out-of-three" rule, 77, 93–95

Web sites, 74n.3

Whitestone, Heather, 19

word order, 46; in ASL, 54

World Federation of the Deaf, 74n.2

World Games for the Deaf, 66–67

World Recreation Association of the Deaf, 67

World Wide Web, ASL on, 69, 74n.3

Zawolkow, Esther, 85